Francis and Kaiora Tipene are the prop a New Zealand funeral business based in Onehunga and Henderson, Auckland. Both hail from Northland, New Zealand – Francis from Pawarenga, Kaiora from Kaitāia. The now married couple met at Māori Teacher's Training College before embarking on a life devoted to their passion for helping people at times of great need.

In 2018 they starred in the first season of what *The Spinoff* called 'the greatest local comedy of 2018', *The Casketeers*, now in its fourth season.

Francis is a graduate of the WelTec Funeral Directors course and started in the industry over fifteen years ago, working as a duty driver in Auckland. Kaiora is also a qualified funeral director.

Tikanga

Living with the traditions of te ao Māori

Authors of the bestseller *Life as a Casketeer*

with Paul Little

HarperCollins*Publishers*

HarperCollins*Publishers*
Australia • Brazil • Canada • France • Germany • Holland • Hungary
India • Italy • Japan • Mexico • New Zealand • Poland • Spain • Sweden
Switzerland • United Kingdom • United States of America

First published in 2021
by HarperCollins*Publishers* (New Zealand) Limited
Unit D1, 63 Apollo Drive, Rosedale, Auckland 0632, New Zealand
harpercollins.co.nz

Copyright © Francis and Kaiora Tipene 2021

Francis and Kaiora Tipene assert the moral right to be identified as the authors of this work. This work is copyright. All rights reserved. No part of this publication may be reproduced, copied, scanned, stored in a retrieval system, recorded, or transmitted, in any form or by any means, without the prior written permission of the publisher.

A catalogue record for this book is available from the National Library of New Zealand.

ISBN 978 1 7755 4175 2 (pbk)
ISBN 978 1 7754 9206 1 (ebook)

Cover design by Micaela Alcaino
Cover photography by Qiane Matata-Sipu
Typeset in Minion Pro by Kelli Lonergan
Printed and bound in Australia by McPherson's Printing Group
The papers used by HarperCollins in the manufacture of this book are a natural, recyclable product made from wood grown in sustainable plantation forests. The fibre source and manufacturing processes meet recognised international environmental standards, and carry certification.

CONTENTS

	Introduction	vii
1.	Being Māori	1
2.	Pepeha	10
3.	Whakapapa	19
4.	Whānau, Hapū and Iwi	31
5.	Kawa and Tikanga	37
6.	Mahi	48
7.	Tangi	58
8.	Tapu and Noa	69
9.	Manaakitanga	81
10.	Kaitiakitanga	94
11.	Mana	100
12.	Hongi	110
13.	Taonga	117
14.	Moko	128
15.	Utu	135
16.	Koha	141
17.	Te Reo Māori	149
18.	Kai	162
19.	Heroes	175
20.	Whaikōrero	185
21.	Whakataukī	199

22. Waiata	208
23. Kapa Haka	219
24. Tāne and Wāhine	230
25. Tamariki	240
26. Rongoā	248
27. Death and Dying	257
28. The Media	262
29. Tauiwi	270
30. Religion	285
31. Business	295
32. Te Tiriti	303

INTRODUCTION

FRANCIS
Ko Makora te maunga
Ko Rotokākahi te awa
Ko Whangapē te moana
Ko Taiao te marae
Ko *Ngātokimatawhaorua* te waka

KAIORA
Ko Te Rangi Aniwaniwa me Puwheke ngā maunga
Ko Rangaunu te moana
Ko Waimanoni te marae
Ko *Māmari* te waka

Not long after our TV series *The Casketeers* first aired in New Zealand, strangers started turning up at our funeral home.

The first people just wanted to look at the place they had seen on TV. Some were surprised to find it was a real funeral home and not a TV studio set. They would bring out their cameras and take a selfie and head off again.

But after a while, they started turning up with questions as well as cameras. One of the things our show does is demonstrate tikanga Māori — the Māori ways of doing things. Somehow, we had ended up being seen as experts on tikanga.

These visitors wanted information, like how to do things correctly according to Māori protocol, or what would be the right phrase to use on a special occasion, or just how to spell a word and whether whānau had a macron on it. We thought that was really beautiful.

We realised there are many people — Pākehā and Māori — who know a little bit about tikanga Māori and would like to know a lot more.

And that is why we have made this book — to describe how tikanga works in our lives and how other people can make it part of their lives if they want to.

* * *

This is not an encyclopaedia of Māori culture. It's not a book of Māori rituals. It's not a phrasebook that you can use to learn some te reo Māori. There are lots of places where you can look up the definition of whānau, hapū or iwi. In this book, we are talking about what those things mean to us.

It is about how these concepts affect us from day to day and how we learnt about them growing up. It won't tell you what you would learn if you were studying them at university, but it will give you an idea of what it is like to have these things be a part of how you think. Many of the examples we use are filtered through the processes surrounding death, since that is our profession and something we deal with every day.

We are not experts in tikanga. We are two people of Māori

Introduction

(and Tongan and Scottish and Scandinavian and other) heritage who were lucky enough to be raised in Māori traditions. Any knowledge we have reflects what we learnt and were exposed to when we were growing up. In most cases, we are still learning.

The views of the topics we talk about here are entirely our own — an explanation of how they fit in our lives. Many of them will be different for other people and other iwi. There are many wiser kaumātua and kuia than us who could give you more thorough versions of these topics.

So, this book is not meant to be the last word on anything. It is meant to be a starting point for all those whose interest in te reo Māori and tikanga has been inspired by what they have seen and read about our work and our lives. Our greatest wish is that it will encourage people to learn more about and share in our culture.

ONE

BEING MĀORI

We identify as Māori. It is our identity.
It tells us where we fit in a world of billions of people.

FRANCIS

For my wife, Kaiora, and myself, our culture is quite simply who we are. We identify as Māori. It is our identity. It tells us where we fit in a world of billions of people. We have shared it for four years now on TV.

In that time, there have been lots of misunderstandings. I have heard people refer to us as 'the Polynesian funeral directors' or 'the brown ones'. Fine. We are associated with Polynesia and we are located in the Pacific, but whatever people call it, what they are seeing on our show is our Māori culture and identity.

KAIORA

I believe that being Māori comes down to a sense of belonging and connection. I was lucky growing up. My parents knew so much tikanga, which they instilled in us as children. I take what I can from that and apply it where I can in our mahi every day.

I've met quite a few urban Māori who have lived all their lives in cities and among Pākehā, and who feel they aren't entitled to belong to their culture. They are suffering because they were not raised with tikanga values. There is still something missing and they really feel that.

These conversations have always been at a funeral. People feel they can connect to their whānau more through death and tangihanga. And they often say, 'I hope we don't just connect back at funerals.'

The growth of urban marae has helped fill this gap, giving Māori in cities a place where they can experience their culture. I have a lot of friends who have graduated or gone through Hoani Waititi Marae in Auckland. Even though they were brought up in Auckland, they are really knowledgeable in terms of their tikanga and have developed a sense of belonging and identity. They have been encouraged to go back to their tūrangawaewae — to their home marae, wherever that might be — and reconnect.

A generation has come through this process, many people who are now employed as tikanga advisers at places like Māori Television. Our kaumātua and kuia who are slowly coming to the end of their times have taught these young people — and we are learning from this new generation ourselves. Francis and I rely on this younger generation to assist us.

FRANCIS
Some people have been worried that the old traditions are being lost. It's good that they are worried. That means they will do something about it.

BEING MĀORI

A couple of generations ago, the old people were extremely worried. Now they are probably feeling a bit more confident. Back then, they didn't have all New Zealand watching a show like *The Casketeers* on TV at 7 p.m. They would have thought that idea was incredible.

Now the culture is being shared more widely.

It is funny that it has taken so long to come up with something that brings Māori values and regular day-to-day tikanga to everyone in the country. Not everyone can go on a marae and learn there. Not everyone grows up around Māori people and gets that exposure. Our show gets across the same message. It shows how things could be.

Every time we do a new show, I ask myself three things: Are we being respectful? Are we using te reo Māori eloquently and subtly? Are we teaching? I hope people are learning something from our show.

It is also strange that it has taken a programme about death to make this entertaining for people. But it was the right platform. People watch and get sad, then during the sadness they learn about the marae, hongi, tangi, waiata, kawa, tikanga and other aspects of the culture.

It has also been great for people overseas — I sometimes wonder if too great, when they have shown up at the door wanting to take their selfies. That has been one good thing about Covid — no random international visitors at the door. We have had to explain that this is a real funeral home. They thought it was a set. Sometimes, if we had time, I took them through to the chapel or showed them the caskets.

I like to make sure we are inclusive on the show. That is why when we do things I try to explain why we do them — and why we don't do other things. The rules and regulations and protocols make up our identity and uniqueness. Everything has a whakapapa and a meaning.

The culture is also changing. And it is not just young people making this happen. The old people know it has to change if it is going to survive. They keep the balance. They know so much about the old ways and their meaning — they will tell us what is important and they know where we can make changes to fit in with the modern world.

This came to mind recently at a tangi at home in Pawarenga. Tangihanga aren't what they used to be. When my pop died, we had to get food for all the people who would be coming. We killed three pigs, two cows and some sheep but, actually, could have managed with half a beef, half a sheep and a pig head for the brawn. A lot of our older generation say this is too hard and we should change; that we actually don't need to have the pig shot.

Manuhiri numbers at events are dwindling now, so it is time to adjust tikanga and think of other ways to do things. We are a long way away from being reduced to a sandwich and a cup of tea. But what won't change is the fact that part of our identity and culture is about feeding people — putting it out there, whether it is all the beef, mutton and pork and going into a bit of debt, or just making some sandwiches.

The important thing is that we have some kai at the end of the funeral. We have to eat to take away the tapu so that we can be in a state of noa and normality after dealing with death.

KAIORA

Our culture needs to be shared with other people if it is going to survive. My father was one who was always about sharing knowledge. He loved sharing it with anyone, even if you weren't Māori. Once he got started sharing, it could be hard to stop him! He would open his door to anyone, no matter where you were from. He was the right person to take you anywhere in the north and could tell you about all the places. He believed you weren't allowed to speak on the marae unless you could whakapapa back to the marae. If you could, then you were allowed to speak.

FRANCIS

Some of us Māori are not very inclusive. I know this from European funeral directors who have been growled at for doing the wrong thing when taking bodies onto marae. It's a bit different when you are in business. You can't afford to be offended if people do the wrong thing. They might seem to be rude or disrespectful, but it is just that they don't know the rules. So we don't complain. But if someone asks us what to do, of course we will point them in the right direction.

We as a culture can decide to be inclusive and that's what I'm about. It's so beautiful then. A lot of Māori expect non-Māori to know the rules: you're a New Zealander, so you should know. But they don't, and I really want us to be able to share. The culture is so beautiful.

But there is a difference between sharing something and giving it away.

I love to share, especially customs to do with funerals. Recently, we did a funeral for a family who didn't have an ounce of Māori in them but, like a lot of Pākehā now, were trying to incorporate some of our practices to help with their grieving.

We transferred this man to his home and I noticed that photos of him had been put around the room, along with some greenery, similar to what we would do on a marae. I had done my job and was about to walk out but it felt incomplete without a karakia. I wasn't quite sure what to do.

Two of the relatives had left the room when the body was brought in. It was a bit of a shock to them, although it's what I'm used to in our culture. If you want to take your loved one home, you embrace them, but I knew this was their way of grieving because they were having trouble accepting things.

Everyone who was left in the room was towards the back — away from the body. I sensed this was the first time they had had a loved one in their home. As I was walking out, the wife hugged me and said, 'Thank you so much. That is my husband in there, but I'm not used to this. Have we put the photos up right and the leaves?'

'You know what?' I said. 'It's beautiful that you have done this.'

'We love Māori culture but we don't know how to do things.'

'Would you mind if we had a karakia?' I said.

'Oh please, could you?'

So they all came together as a whānau for a karakia. The wife just wanted something similar to Māori cultural ways in their home for that moment. They didn't continue on with all the other tikanga, but what they did do made them feel better and it made for a better experience.

The Pākehā way of dealing with death is totally different from what I've been brought up with, but it's not about me.

Every time we do a new show, I ask myself three things: Are we being respectful? Are we using te reo Māori eloquently and subtly? Are we teaching?

I accept people are how they are and do things in their own way. When I was first learning the funeral industry and found out that Pākehā loved ones stayed at the funeral director's till the day of the funeral, and that people didn't come to see them, I couldn't understand it.

But we will keep them at our premises if that's what people want. And we do a waiata for them and say goodnight because we are responsible for them if they are with us and the family isn't there. I have to get used to it. It is their way of tangi. We will have a sing-song, a karakia, and when we do get to the funeral I tell the family, 'Mum has been behaving. She has been doing our waiata,' and they love it.

Everyone needs to respect everyone else's culture — sometimes you do that by not trying to share it.

For a long time, Māori culture was put in the background. But there were still people carrying this knowledge around, with no idea of what might happen to it in generations to come. Luckily, a younger urban generation was interested in preserving it.

My own family was part of the big migration of people moving to the cities for work. Everyone was going to work for power boards and so on. They cared about paying the bills more than they cared about their identity. Māori families across Auckland tried to have little wānanga in that setting. They had te reo classes and haka classes. They had gatherings for reviving waiata. They would talk about anything and everything, usually with a bit to drink.

These things were done to keep the culture alive, because it was evident if things kept going the way they were, Māori would be gone. But there were leaders within groups like the power board and other workplaces who had the idea to come together.

They did this at the Auckland Māori Community Centre in downtown Auckland. But it also happened at school halls and other places where people could congregate.

They passed on the knowledge through oratory — you were expected to hear it and take it in. Many of us now like to write it down, because that is easier with so much else going on in our heads and our lives.

The elders had the foresight to see that if we didn't do anything, our language, our pepeha and our identity would be gone before they knew it. Thank goodness they did. Those elders have gone on but their knowledge has been left to their whānau. I'm so grateful for that.

TWO

PEPEHA

A pepeha names your tribe, your parents, the mountain, river, lake and ocean associated with them, and the waka that carried your first ancestors to arrive in New Zealand, around 1000 years ago.

FRANCIS

At the start of this book, we have put our pepeha. This is a simple way of telling people who you are and where you are from. It names your tribe, your parents, the mountain, river, lake and ocean associated with them, and the waka that carried your first ancestors to arrive in New Zealand, around 1000 years ago.

One of the most important things about a pepeha is that it enables you to connect with other people. When you hear someone's pepeha and they mention the same maunga as yours then you know you have a connection. You may even have some of the same tūpuna.

I first learnt mine at kōhanga reo in Pawarenga, from the beautiful kuia there: Nanny Bubby, Nanny Olive, Nanny Daphne.

After kai and the sandpit and waiata, we learnt about the maunga and the whakapapa.

Reflecting back on that, I think I've missed something with my own children who haven't had that experience. I remember learning it like it was yesterday. You do learn it when those old kuia teach you. At the time, the maunga and the awa and the other parts of the pepeha didn't mean much. 'Okay. Now we'll go back to the trucks and the sandpit.' But thanks to them we understood these things by the time we finished primary school. They set you up for life. I'm a bit sad for my kids, but hopefully it is never too late to get them sorted.

When you said, 'Ko Makora, my maunga,' that mountain was right on your doorstep. You gazed up at it and it looked massive. Then the awa Rotokākahi, then the marae Taiao. They are all associated with kōhanga reo for me. My sons will be doing it in Auckland, which is okay, but when you do it at home up north, you can point directly to everything — there is your mountain, there is your marae. It means a lot more than teaching them here in Tāmaki Makaurau.

I'm stirred to get that going now. We do a lot of karakia and hīmene at home, but we have forgotten our tūrangawaewae, and about grounding our children and teaching them how they hono back to their home.

I explain a pepeha by comparing it to the ID card you show when you get pulled over. Except instead of having it on a card, you do it through oratory. As soon as you start your pepeha or your whakapapa, you hear people going, 'Ahhhhh ...' in recognition. Yes, we should take each other at face value and love everyone, but things change once you are able to make a direct connection.

When you hear someone's pepeha and they mention the same maunga as yours then you know you have a connection. You may even have some of the same tūpuna.

There are still some kaumātua left with an amazing amount of knowledge but not as many as there used to be. Pā Henare Tate at Hato Petera was like a walking encyclopaedia. He could whakapapa anyone back if he knew their name. When I first started at that school, he said to me, 'Ngā Tipene nō? You're the Tipene from where?'

'From Panguru.'

'Ah — ko Mike Tipene mā.' And so on. He knew it all.

We quite often get confused with other Tipene families; when you tell people you're the Tipene from Panguru, they're still not sure. But Pā Tate knew what the connection was.

KAIORA

I love hearing pepeha. I love hearing the names of places I haven't heard of before. I can go and google it and find out all about it. When an individual stands and gives out their pepeha, you know what they are referring to.

It's different from your whakapapa, where you list your connections through the generations. It's a shortcut to connecting with a person.

You start with your awa, then your maunga, your waka, your tangata — which is your tūpuna — then your marae, your hapū, your iwi, and then you say your parents and then you.

I learnt that at kōhanga reo, where we did our pepeha every day and finished with a kai. But when I went to primary school, because there was no kura kaupapa for me to attend, it was all very different. And I was made to feel different.

The teacher just read our names out from a roll. I wanted to do my pepeha.

'Can I show you what we did at kōhanga reo?' I asked the teacher. She said okay and I did my pepeha. She asked me what it all meant and I told her.

'Okay, well, thank you very much,' said the teacher. 'Every morning we will call the roll out and you just answer.'

At kōhanga reo, you told people who you were with your pepeha. At regular school, they told you who you were. Like it was their decision.

I missed standing up every day to tell people who I was. I forgot how to say a pepeha. I must have been in standard three when I was in a bilingual unit and they said, 'You've got to know your whakapapa and pepeha.' I had forgotten it, but I was excited that I could learn it again.

There were moments when it all came back to me. I was putting my hand up, excited — 'I know! I can say it!'

When I finished, my mates were impressed. 'Bro, that was cool,' said one.

Connections were quickly established.

'You have the same maunga as me,' said another.

'Yeah?'

'Out in Awanui. Hey, we must be cousins.'

'What's your name and I'll go back and tell my dad.' I did and my dad said this kid was actually my nephew.

Our own kids have been brought up differently from us, and I have been a bit shocked to realise they are not as advanced in their culture as we were at their age. I understood their teachers had taught our children their pepeha. One got his maunga and his marae confused. But I would put that responsibility back on us as parents. After all, we know their pepeha better than their teachers do.

At school, they were given a pepeha sheet. It's a famous one I've seen in every beginners' classroom. It has a picture of a mountain, a picture of a marae and so on. Kids bring it home and colour it in.

I don't know if the other kids in their class would have been able to fill it out. Perhaps not, if they are not connected to local iwi in some way. I hope their parents would have used initiative to say their home is their marae — whatever street it is. A lot of people would use their Toyota as a waka. That's not lying or disrespecting anything cultural. It is just telling people where they are from.

FRANCIS

Generally, when we take a tūpāpaku back to the family or the marae or are doing introductions, it is good first of all to introduce yourself. A lot of times, I don't know the dead person or their family. And if they need a speaker for the marae, it is usually me if there is no one else there. So I need to identify myself. I use the pepeha and that sets things up.

When it comes to naming my father, I use my grandfather's name. That means no disrespect to my father, but he is Tongan and the people listening wouldn't know his name. But they would recognise my grandfather's Māori name — Walter (or Waata) Tipene — and he brought me up so I am entitled to use it.

What people are looking for — especially away from home — is a way to connect you to the hapū or iwi. 'Ah, he's a Tipene from up north.' That also means that if you make any mistakes, they understand. If you are in a Tūhoe or Waikato setting, for example, where the people are strict about these things, they will make allowances: 'Oh well, he is from the north and they are different in terms of how the kawa is said.'

Pepeha can have other side effects, too. I was very impressed with my wife's connections when I found out she was Tainui. These connections open you up to people. Especially down there, where they are so strong. My wife was already royalty to me, but it turned out she was Tainui royalty as well.

I thought she was all about Pawarenga and Kaitāia until she told me, weeks into our relationship, that her mum is actually from Tainui.

'Are you Waikato?' I asked. I was a bit astonished.

'Yeah. Nanaia Mahuta is my mum's cousin.'

'Are you kidding?'

'Incredibly distant, but yeah. My grandmother's brother was a spokesman for Dame Te Atairangikaahu.'

'Oh my gosh! Am I going to marry royalty?'

That cracked her up so much. 'Bro, I'm more Ngāpuhi than anything.'

'Yeah, but you are part of Kīngitanga — you can go back there any time.'

* * *

I have heard some Māori say Pākehā have no right to do pepeha for themselves but I think it could be a beautiful thing — a good tradition for both cultures to have.

It is different for Europeans, of course. They like to talk about how long they have been here, almost in a competitive way.

At kōhanga reo, you told people who you were with your pepeha. At regular school, they told you who you were.

Māori don't talk about how long we've been here. We've always been here. All of us.

But most Pākehā at least live near a mountain that they could name in a pepeha. My wife and I live in a suburb that is named after the maunga at its centre: Mt Eden or Maungawhau.

If our Pākehā children and our Māori children are being brought up in these areas, have a home there, go to school there, then the powers-that-be should encourage their schools to give these mountains in their pepeha. And there is a usually a stream or other body of water somewhere nearby. For instance, Aucklanders all share the Waitematā Harbour.

If Onehunga Primary School does a pepeha to One Tree Hill Primary School, both have the same mountain. They will find they are connected by doing their pepeha. And kids being kids, if they find out they share a mountain, lake or river they will be excited. The relationship will be strengthened.

The next step is the whakapapa, tracing all our family connections, people coming down the line then back up again, all the way to the original two people up there.

THREE

WHAKAPAPA

When it comes to people, whakapapa is not just about being able to find blood connections. It is also about building relationships.

KAIORA

I have always been taught the primary aspect of whakapapa is that someone has come from somewhere. Everyone belongs to something, and you can connect to that person. I love when people stand up and do mihi and acknowledge their maunga and awa. 'Oh, that is my maunga and awa, too. I wonder if they know this person that I know.' Now you are about to build a relationship. You have heard of that iwi and can connect to it through mutual friends.

Everything has a hono — a connection with something else. Even objects have whakapapa. People have whakapapa connecting them to their tūpuna going back in time, but also whakapapa that goes sideways — to cousins and others of their generation.

My dad was obsessed with whakapapa. It was impossible for him to not find the connections between things. It could be a hat, a chair or a kete. He knew that someone had made them — they had put a lot of work into them. That is the whakapapa of those things. The kete didn't come out of nothing.

Even a coffee cup from The Warehouse has a whakapapa. It is made out of clay, so it comes from the earth, from Papatūānuku. The clay was brought out of the ground, moulded and put into the fire, which also has a whakapapa that we acknowledge when we talk about Rūaumoko, the god of volcanic rock.

A lot of things went into making the cup appear and were added to its DNA. It didn't just come from the shop where we paid our $5. Human hands touched it along the way. Knowing it has a whakapapa reminds us of the beautiful message that everything in the world is connected somehow or other.

A kete is made out of muka, fibre taken from the flax. Someone has carefully chosen that flax, picked one colour out of all the other colours. She has taken it back to her house, peeled it back to reveal the fine fibres inside and used them to make the kete.

Because I know that whakapapa, every time I see someone with one of those kete, I am impressed — I know what has gone into making it and where it has come from.

When it comes to people, whakapapa is not just about being able to find blood connections. It is also about building relationships.

When people came over to our house, my dad didn't like not knowing who they were. He would always ask their name.

'Oh, are you so-and-so's son?'

'Yeah, I am.'

'Well, how is Uncle Blah Blah?'

'Who?'

'Your uncle.'

'I'm not sure if that's my uncle.'

'Yes, that's your uncle, man.'

And then he brought out his book. My father had a lot of books containing information about his tūpuna and their lines of generation. If he wasn't doing much, he would go back to a book, look for a name and see how far he could go to connect to it, and who was still alive of that lineage.

And he told the person where they were from. My sisters got so embarrassed. They brought a boy home to say hello and suddenly he was getting a whakapapa lesson. Actually, they stopped bringing boys home for that reason. Maybe that was my dad's plan all along.

If my father were alive and knew about Francis and me, he would say, 'Put him back. We don't want it.' Because there was bad blood between our family and some people at Pawarenga where Francis is from. Even though Francis wasn't directly connected to the problem, we could whakapapa to it.

My last name is Murray, which is from a Scottish side I am still to learn about. Many aunties and uncles have researched this — gone back to Scotland itself and learnt about our tūpuna.

To my dad, it didn't matter which culture you were from, he would somehow make a connection. He could go back to all waka. And we all come off some waka, at some point, so he would make you feel like you were whānau.

He also taught us that you don't just go back for five generations in a straight line. All those people had brothers and sisters and children and their brothers and sisters and children. It's not just about how many generations you can go back, it's about how you can connect yourself through your bloodline to other people.

He wasn't so hard on us younger ones. Older ones had to whakapapa back so many generations of a particular aunty or uncle and how we were connected, so when we went back to our own marae, or maybe another one, he would always say, 'This is your uncle — his grandfather and my grandfather were brothers.' We might not know how a cousin was related so he got us to learn our own genealogy. There would be a lesson every Sunday. I was probably eight or nine when I memorised that:

> When my great-grandfather came here from Scotland, he married a princess named Kataraina Te Koni from Te Aupōuri. Then they had Karaihe Murray who married Akanihi Puku. They had Tuakana Murray who married Marara Mete from Mangamuka. They had Hirikia Tuakana Murray who married Katie Awarau from Awanui. Then Hani Murray who married Ruana, my mum, and then they had me.
>
> Mete was my great-grandmother. She is in line to Mangamuka and Hilda Harawira, Hone's wife's mother — her name is Marara Murray and she is named after our tūpuna.

We also had to learn Mum's side but we didn't do so well there. I could go back maybe three generations. I should attend some wānanga in Kīngitanga land to inform myself about these connections. I know Francis would enjoy learning more about our links to royalty.

One of the reasons my dad went to so much trouble to teach us was that he didn't want us going into an environment and not knowing if a certain person was an uncle or other relative.

The primary aspect of whakapapa is that someone has come from somewhere. Everyone belongs to something, and you can connect to that person.

It would always bring a tear to his eye if he could connect to people. He would have a little tangi when he realised that.

In his last years, he was sick with diabetes and he needed lots of attention. He wasn't very mobile and I became his helper. That required me to be away from school a lot. And away from other kids a lot, too, because, instead of being out playing, I had to help him.

'Don't go too far, Kaiora. Daddy needs you.'

That was the last four years of his life for me. We went to every marae and hui he wanted to go to. It was a bit boring but I had no option, and now I'm grateful for those last moments in his life, because I learnt a lot about whānau and iwi, who we are and where we come from. That was a big education in whakapapa.

We travelled a lot. I often found myself waking up not sure where I was. We would be in Pakanae or Rāwhiti, and there was Dad, sitting there having a cup of tea with people I'd never seen before. On the way home he would say, 'You know that person in there? He is first cousin to your grandfather.' We travelled all that way to find that out? Ka pai, Dad.

FRANCIS

What would the Pākehā equivalent to whakapapa be? Ultimately, everything goes back to Io Matua, the supreme being. For that reason, I feel Pākehā can have a sense of connection to Papatūānuku, too. It may be a place in Europe. Surely they have a history somewhere that can be connected back to Mother Earth.

Pākehā might start doing it a bit more, the way they have adopted parts of other Māori traditions. We find out our whakapapa by talking to people. Pākehā find theirs out by going into the library and spending hours going through shipping records from the nineteenth century.

Some Pākehā are very excited to be able to say their families have been here since 1830 or before. But Māori never have to say that. We have all been here that long, and no one has been here longer than anyone else's ancestors because they all came at the same time. Pākehā ask each other questions like: Who are your people and where did they go to school? Or: Which boat did your people come over on? Hierarchy and status are important in both cultures. Maybe we share similar concerns but show them in different ways. People like to be able to say they are connected to this rangatira or that lord. I know I have a bit of Swedish on my father's side.

Whakapapa is not just about blood links. It includes other kinds of connection. If you have an association with someone, it has real and practical effects. If you are my friend, you would be entitled to rock up to my marae and say, 'Hello, I'm a friend of Francis's from Auckland.'

'Oh — a friend of Francis's? Haere mai. Come in.'

Whakapapa can be present even if there is no blood link. For example, through friendship: perhaps my great-grandfather and your great-grandfather were best mates. Or someone might have had a mistress and that is another connection. We can connect through mishaps in life. Your grandmother and mine were sisters, even though you didn't know about it. Or there was a whāngai many years ago when this kuia looked after my mother and you are part of the kuia's family.

We have Maggie from Fiji here, helping to look after our kids. I might go to Fiji in 20 years and meet one of her cousins and we can explain that connection. I hear it time and again in speeches at tangi: 'Your grandfather lived next door to us and we worked together on the Power Board.' Those are memories that connect people using stories. In a roomful of people, we think we don't know anyone but we want to connect. We want to be able to relate to people we don't know because it is human nature to want to be cared for and recognised and humanly connected.

I love how in death we are united and come together, and that all comes down to whakapapa.

I form relationships with people when I do funerals for them. In fact, a time of grief is probably one of the best times to build a relationship. If you are there for someone in their most vulnerable moments, you establish a connection with them. You become connected with all of them because you have looked after one of their loved ones. You are now whānau to them.

You are not just someone who works at a funeral home. They will get up and do a mihi to you in their final funeral service. They acknowledge you, and that is really humbling.

The disputes over where someone should be buried, which sometimes occur, are a good example of where whakapapa has a very practical function. Knowing the connections helps you decide where someone belongs and where their body should go.

Wherever you go — on any marae — there always seems to be someone knowledgeable who can whakapapa and connect you. It can turn into a long discussion that needs a couple of nights and turns up skeletons in the closet. I have run into a few where I couldn't believe what I was hearing — even cases of murder.

Some of the things people did in the past can be affecting what happens to you today. People are still hated for what someone else did back then.

There is one case where I am close to a whānau but there is some raruraru from back in history. I know if anyone in that whānau dies they will take him to the opposition for the funeral. That is how that stuff carries on.

If you set off on a whakapapa journey, you have to be prepared for that sort of thing. But there are more beautiful things than nasty ones.

Also, we are more open to the LGBT+ community now. In the past, it wasn't like that and lots of bad things happened to whānau who were that way inclined. May they rest in peace. What a life they must have lived. But look at where we are now.

KAIORA

Knowing your whakapapa means you know your connections when you go on a marae. You can connect to particular aunties and uncles and feel proud. And as you sit there during a hui, they will pass on more of their knowledge to you.

But there are ups and downs to that — it brings responsibilities. There are times when you would like to lay back and just listen and learn. But there are times when you can't. You have to do the mihi or the karanga or waiata. If your aunty is going to the toilet, it's your role to get in and do the karanga, no matter how young you are. 'Aunty won't be long — come over and do the karanga.' They know you can do it because they've taught you. They don't have a problem with you being the one to do it because they know your whakapapa, so they know who you are.

And the opposite is true, if you haven't established the connection, like when I go back up to Waimanoni, where my father and grandmother are from. Even though my roots are there, and

Our old dad did his best to ensure we went to every marae hui — so we knew who was who and whether to call them whānau or friends.

my father is buried there, I haven't spent enough time there or given enough to my iwi or marae to be able to call it home.

I can go back and do a karanga or fit into those roles, but I don't feel I have earned that right.

It's not enough just to know your connection. You have to have lived it as well.

It is different for one of my sisters. She has given a lot to the marae. She attends the hui. She does fundraisers for them. The rest of us acknowledge her for keeping the fires burning up there. You must be living there if you want the role, the mana or to have a say in things. It would be like a Pākehā turning up to a castle in England and saying, 'G'day, cuz.'

I try to instil some of this in our kids. About once a year, we have a whānau gathering for my mum's side. It's for our immediate family, but there are twelve siblings and we all have kids. We are multiplying. My boys haven't seen their extended whānau for some time and we are still having new babies so it is important they know who they are. There are four nephews in Australia who have had probably six children between them, and who we haven't met yet.

I hope my boys will meet them soon. Later in life, they might get a job and be working with a nephew or cousin and not know it.

That is why our old dad did his best to ensure we went to every marae hui — so we knew who was who and whether to call them whānau or friends. We knew who our immediate family were. It was wrong if we didn't know our cousins. Now I'm feeling a bit whakamā that I know all my first cousins on both sides but not much about their children.

Growing up, I was grateful to learn how to trace our family back five generations to our tupuna John Alfred Borrowdale, who came from Scotland. His descendants are all over the country.

I met an artist who had been back to Scotland to look into his family, and when I heard about it, I thought, 'It sounds like he is learning about me. I better let him know we might be cousins.'

He was buzzy when I contacted him. 'You're from that show.'

'Yes, and you're that artist who goes around Tauranga and puts things up.'

'Yeah, sis, we can hook up some time and talk about a few things.'

He had come back with so much knowledge about our ancestor in Scotland. He said he felt complete now, because he knew where he came from on all sides. I felt envious in a way. I would like to go to Scotland some time and learn where my tūpuna lived and how they lived.

FOUR

WHĀNAU, HAPŪ AND IWI

*Whānau, hapū and iwi are an important part of whakapapa.
That is why they would be hard to dissolve.
That system is integrated into our being.*

FRANCIS

We all belong to a whānau, a hapū and an iwi.

A whānau is a family. A whānau organises itself. My address is a house on such and such a street. I might live on Pawarenga Road at this certain postcode — and so that's my address and that's where I will raise and mentor and love and nourish my own whānau as I see fit.

But I also belong to a bigger address, which is the hapū at Pawarenga. The whole of Pawarenga is the subtribe of our iwi, Te Rarawa. The beautiful thing about a hapū is that, hopefully, your little whānau goals and tikanga fit with the iwi and big picture.

In the hapū, you still have your individuality. When I go onto a marae people will say, 'Oh, there's Francis from the Pawarenga Valley hapū.' Same iwi, different subtribes.

As a hapū, we do things differently. There is a tikanga for the marae in the north and there are slight changes between the hapū. They adapt it slightly to suit their own needs.

Whānau, hapū and iwi, especially, are an important part of whakapapa. That is why they would be hard to dissolve. That system is already integrated into our being. It is part of our kōrero in our pepeha and whakapapa, when we share it through speech and conversation. That is why it is so easy to talk about.

A beautiful thing up north is that we are very community oriented. We have three marae in Pawarenga, which all belong to Te Uri o Tai hapū and are of Te Rarawa iwi. They get together and have an annual sports day for the hapū. It is a fundraiser for all three marae. The people come to Pawarenga and buy food and T-shirts and raffle tickets and so on to help cover the expenses of the marae.

In that way, the hapū of the Te Rarawa iwi are doing their bit to sustain themselves. They are not relying on the iwi to pay for everything. I love that.

When we sell the T-shirts and jerseys, it is a way to express our identity. It is a chance to show we are proud of our hapū, even when there are so many bad things going on. A lot of Aucklanders come, and when they buy the T-shirts and other merchandise, that makes people proud. If I see someone wearing one of those tops when I am back in Auckland, I am overwhelmed.

These structures are the answer to a lot of problems Māori have. Iwi are or should be in charge of social services. During the Covid-19 lockdowns, they laid out kai and did the shopping and deliveries and ensured pastoral care of kuia and kaumātua in their community. They transported people to town for their shopping or picked up their prescriptions and brought their medicines to them. It was a wonderful example of how the system our ancestors created works perfectly. It has survived colonisation and racist structures and all sorts of other obstacles being imposed on it.

My whānau and hapū have our own raruraru — every whānau and hapū does. But when things got tough through Covid, they were there. My grandmother had to turn away some of the kai that people brought her. There was too much. It was more than she could eat. That was wonderful.

In all fairness, things were so different from normal but people pulled together. That is what I loved about it. The big picture is all about that. Organising our whānau properly. Everyone was there and connected and ready to go. I love that model, when it is working right. We need to get the right people elected to keep this happening.

Iwi have solutions to the iwi's problems. You hear a lot of sad stories on the news about things like child welfare and Oranga Tamariki. Iwi have the bigger picture for that, which involves giving children who are at risk back to their whānau, hapū and iwi.

That's one example of Māori dealing with Māori problems. Those solutions won't be perfect or always better, but they will take place inside a structure that works.

In any system, you will get people who are crooks. You will get people with their own agendas, people with ambitions to get into politics later and wanting to get themselves a reputation now. But there are safeguards against that in the system. This is why we have representatives from hapū and iwi on rūnanga or councils — so that there is a wide representation of all people.

The whānau is the core unit, the hapū is your extended family and the iwi is your extended, extended whānau. My whānau is Dad, Mum and twelve siblings. That has always been my whānau.

You also hear bad things about some iwi and what happens to the money they get in compensation for the land they lost, for instance. When that amount falls into their hands, there is so much of it that, usually, some will go missing. That is where we need to have strong people in charge. Big iwi like Ngāi Tahu and Tainui are used to dealing with the big sums, but if you chuck all this to tribes who aren't used to those amounts you need the right people to control it. I am all for iwi governing themselves but we need the right skill sets. Our hiccups are the same as other institutions, but they get more mentions in the media.

KAIORA
Another way of putting it is that the whānau is the core unit, the hapū is your extended family and the iwi is your extended, extended whānau. The hapū or iwi is not defined by the number of people in it. My whānau is Dad, Mum and twelve siblings. That has always been my whānau. Now they are multiplying. We all have kids. It's a big whānau. Suddenly, there are more than forty of us. You could say that the Murray lot are now their own hapū. But we are still a whānau who belong to a hapū. That hapū is Ngāti Māhanga of Waikato, my mother's area. Wherever we are from, that is the hapū of our iwi.

Growing up, we learnt about Muriwhenua, which is not an iwi but a defined area made up of iwi in the Far North. The furthest iwi north is Ngati Kuri. There is another iwi from maybe Te Kao down to Awanui. Then Ngāi Takoto where my dad is buried. Although the boundaries between these areas aren't always clear.

There always has been some debate about exactly what the Muriwhenua is, but Dad taught me that we have our Murray blood through all of them. That's one reason we spent all that time visiting so many marae establishing connections. He always said, 'Don't connect yourself to just one iwi. You can connect yourself to all the iwi up there.'

A marae in an iwi's area will be connected to that iwi. In some areas, there are borders between the hapū within the iwi, and those hapū will be dominant at particular marae. On the East Coast, they have huge areas where every hapū might have its own marae. It can be hard to connect a hapū to a marae, but it's easy to make the connection to an iwi.

FIVE

KAWA AND TIKANGA

Kawa drives rules about how to behave; it can change from place to place. Tikanga is something you make in your life as you go along; it is based on all the traditions you learnt growing up.

FRANCIS

Kawa and tikanga are two important concepts that are similar but different. They can overlap, and even we can get a bit confused about them sometimes.

A good way to explain it is that both drive rules about how to behave. Kawa can change from place to place, but at each place it will be solid and stay the same. There is more diversity in tikanga and its rules can change a lot more.

Kawa would be that you are not allowed on the marae unless you are called. When you go there with the tūpāpaku for a tangi, you can't walk on till you've had the karanga. Another time, if you go for a meeting there is no karanga. You could say that using cutlery to eat a meal is kawa, but what cutlery you have and how you use it is tikanga.

Kawa can never be changed. You are governed by that. Tikanga is being driven by a set of values that have been preserved.

In the North Island, generally, the Far North, the central and southern areas all have different kawa on their marae. They have their own protocols about how to approach the marae, how to enter, and how to speak and stand when you get there. I've learnt a lot about these regional differences from doing funerals in different parts of the country.

Up north, we gather at the gate, enter, wait for the call, go on, have a prayer, then ask to be seated, and the tangata whenua, who have all stood to greet us, then sit down and hand the mana over to the visitors. We stand and reply, then we all sit down. We do the hongi after that.

Once you know what sort of kawa it is, it will never change. Pāeke is pāeke and you don't mess with such speaking protocols. One of the things that is beautiful about kawa is that it's there wherever you go. Taking a body back — to a home, a marae or a funeral home — will always start with prayer, acknowledging the Lord, speeches afterwards. That never changes. I've never been anywhere that is different.

Tikanga is something you make in your life as you go along. It is based on all the traditions you learnt growing up, but it is adapted to get the best result in the world we live in. The thinking that says, 'This is how we did it, so we must keep doing it that way,' is still out there, but most people acknowledge that the world has changed so much that we need to take the best of the past and make it work for us in the present.

KAIORA

To me, tikanga is summed up in the phrase 'Kei a koe te tikanga', meaning 'it is up to you'. You make your own tikanga. You put down what you want and people will follow. If there is nothing established, it is up to you to put something in place.

In general, I am led by what I have been taught, which is a mix of my dad's rules from home and urban Māori practices.

At the same time, you don't want to takahi or trample all over other people's ways. My dad was all about tradition, but he was all about getting things done, too, which meant sometimes he would even ignore the kawa of a place. A lot of people think marae are all about the standing and waiting, but he was an impatient man. If he thought he was having to wait too long to be called on, he would just begin his karanga and start moving. And he would say why in his karanga: 'You fellas are making my cousin wait. We have come here to see you. Don't make us wait. We are at the gate.'

A good example of how tikanga changes is the difference between how things were when I was a kid and how they are for my kids now. They get away with so much. When a kaumātua got up to speak, you couldn't run in front of him. All we wanted to do was start playing but you couldn't move until his kōrero had finished. You couldn't even run behind him.

When I got a whack on the legs from one of my uncles, with his tokotoko stick, I knew not to talk while he was talking. It was so embarrassing, but my dad didn't feel a bit sorry for me. 'See, I told you,' he said. 'And I'll give you another one when we get in the car.'

I would like to ensure my kids know tikanga marae and tikanga karakia. Of course, they would prefer to be hanging out with their cousins, playing bullrush or rugby, or running after a horse.

Francis's nan allows them to get away with murder. I believe the kaumātua of this generation love our children so much they let them do just about anything. We've been trying to instil in our kids that they should sit still and wait till the kōrero is finished, but it seems to be hard. Especially when the kaumātua are allowing them to play up. The younger three have trouble sitting still for anything. Our two big boys know some tikanga.

That's why keeping in touch with your marae is so important. The more we go home and spend time on our marae, the more our boys learn and understand. One day they will get the message that they can't run around when a karakia is happening, and that bullrush happens on the other side of the fence.

They already know there is a dedicated space for the manuhiri and karanga. If they want Mum's attention, they can't just run on there. The tikanga is that they wait for the kaumātua to finish talking and for the manuhiri to come out. Usually, when the kai is on is the sign that they can start running around and making some noise.

If they go into the kitchen, they have to make themselves useful. They have to peel some potatoes.

This is part of how we educate the younger ones. Back up north, they begin in the kitchen. It is the right place to start and learn. After a while, they make their way into the wharenui to listen and learn. If you can't peel a kūmara, you shouldn't be in the wharenui. So you peel the kūmara first. Get a tea towel. Do some dishes. Then you can go into the wharenui to listen to the korero.

If you can't peel a kūmara, you shouldn't be in the wharenui. So you peel the kūmara first. Get a tea towel. Do some dishes. Then you can go into the wharenui to listen to the korero.

Some people start in the kitchen and never leave. You see them in there and you can tell they're going to stay put because that is where they are happy. Aunty will keep doing the spuds. Uncle will keep doing the meat.

If it is obvious someone is born to be in the kitchen, you can't push them to the front and make them do other things. Go out and look around and find the best people to learn, the ones who have an appetite for that new knowledge.

This principle doesn't just apply to kōrero. It is also true for karakia or for waiata. You can tell who is best to learn the whakapapa, understand the lines at the cemetery, and who will be able to tell you who should be buried where. They will know if a space that looks good for a grave is not the right one because it doesn't belong to this whānau.

The more kids you have, the harder it gets to give them the same level of attention and the same amount of instruction. There was definitely more time to teach the older two.

I think about my dad with these things and wonder how he did it with twelve of us kids. And my mother, sitting behind him like a hen, making sure we didn't go until he had done his kōrero and waiata.

I really didn't like it then, but now I get why he was so strict on us. I'm glad now he was strict. If he hadn't been, I wouldn't have known nearly as much tikanga marae as I do.

He was harder on the older ones than he was on us younger ones. There were just too many of us by then. We were always naughty and would play up on the marae. He gave up. He would just say, 'Get these kids out of here.'

Another important thing about tikanga is that you can't just learn it for one area. You have to learn tikanga for school, home and the marae, but all together because they will all come in contact at some point.

Peer pressure will have an effect on how our kids learn. All kids will want to fit in with their friends, and the world they are moving in will be one where tikanga is observed.

In his last year at primary school, Moronai, who is our second eldest, was very staunch. He was nine or ten and desperate to learn more about tikanga, te reo Māori and haka. He asks to go to kura kaupapa even now. We would like that to happen but organising the travel every day has been a big problem We are working on it.

More recently, I had another case where tikanga came up and I felt it wasn't being observed, so I did something about it. It was at the New Zealand Television Awards, of all things. Mihingarangi Forbes won the overall award for best news and current affairs presenter. It was awesome to see Māori achievement in mainstream awards. For a Māori reporter to get reporter of the year, to be top of the country, was special.

She started her talk and I was disappointed to see no one else there was doing a karanga. You had a lot of Māori people, who should have been examples for achievement and tikanga, in the room. Māori Television were there in full force. Tikanga was that she should be acknowledged, but no one did it. She started her kōrero.

'Right, I'm gonna get up,' I said.

'You get up and you keep going, baby,' said Francis. He knew it wouldn't have made any difference if he had said no.

They say your children are a reflection of you, and I like to believe I'm teaching them some values and to show respect to others.

So I stood up and called out, and when she heard it she stopped speaking. That's tikanga, too — to acknowledge the person doing the karanga. Then Francis busted out a haka and I heard about twenty people behind us get up and do a haka also, and that was cool.

That story shows the two cultures mingling. A few years ago, the Television Awards would have been a completely white ceremony, all done in the Pākehā way and with one Māori winning something. Mihi didn't win a 'Māori award' — she won her award out of all the people present and it needed to be celebrated with karanga and haka. People take this for granted now; there is nothing unusual about it.

* * *

The practice of tikanga isn't something you do consciously. It should be what your whānau does automatically, but sometimes you have to make it happen.

We have family evenings once a week in order to catch up on what we have all done for the past seven days. The kids know the rules for this. We give them all an opportunity to speak and they know only one can talk at a time. They have to stand up and tell us about their day and any problems they have had. No one can talk while they are standing. They are given the mana to have a kōrero.

If a teacher has been in touch and told us one of them has done well at something, we bring it up then. It is uplifting for them as individuals, so they feel empowered in front of their brothers. If they have responsibilities at home or school, it is an opportunity to make sure they are seeing those through.

Tikanga in the home is not just a once-a-week thing, either. I like to have karakia when I wake up to start the day and in the evenings. I always like to have karakia with kai before I eat it. There is an old belief that you might get sick if you don't bless the kai.

I have a thing about brushing hair around the kitchen. My dad always said hair was tapu, so you shouldn't be mingling it with food, because then it becomes noa and he didn't like that feeling. He made it seem like it was really yucky. Sitting on the table was the same sort of thing. You just didn't do it.

I have a pet hate about the boys wearing hats in the house. It's a sign of respect that they don't do that. It's a tikanga I've put in place for them. They say your children are a reflection of you, and I like to believe I'm teaching them some values and to show respect to others.

No shoes inside is an absolute rule. Our kids know not to wear shoes in other people's homes because that is what we do in our home. If we go visiting and they see shoes on in someone's house, they whisper to me because they are a bit shocked. Mihaka gets really frustrated if others can wear shoes and he can't.

'Mum, does that mean I can put my shoes on?'

'No, you can't.'

I love that we teach our kids these things at home, so they then practise them at other people's whare. It makes me proud to see them get up and do the dishes and put the plates away.

It can get a bit complicated. No hats on tables is easy — you just don't put your hat on the table because you have food on the table. But then you have a coffee table — can you put your hat on that? I thought so; it's just decoration.

Mihaka once put his hat on the coffee table.

'Take your hat off there,' said Nikora.

'That's not a table,' said his brother.

'It's okay because we're not going to have kai on it,' said Francis.

'Sometimes baby Francis eats his noodles on it,' said Nikora. Francis didn't know that. He thought Francis junior ate exclusively in the kitchen. Now that it's been exposed, we are going to have a rule to keep the hats and brushes off the coffee table.

The head is very sacred. When we do removals and uplift a body, once it is on the stretcher, we have a plastic covering that sits on top of the head to prevent anything of the zip-up cover touching that face. Also, sometimes the covers are so heavy they can bend your nose. So it has a purpose.

FRANCIS

It was different for us when we were growing up. Sometimes, when I'm upset with the kids, I sound off, 'You don't know what it used to be like. A bit of upbringing with Nana and Pop would have been good for you.' But Nana is soft on them now anyway. Tikanga changes.

SIX

MAHI

To do our job, we need set tikanga that we follow to keep us spiritually safe and the families spiritually settled and in tune. It's tikanga taken over from the marae.

FRANCIS

Everyone with a business thinks theirs is different from other businesses. But I think ours is 'more different' than most. It is especially different because it is so dependent on its culture and being able to live tikanga every day, no matter what else is going on.

Everyone wants to have a gathering when someone dies. They want to unite and have a ceremony for their loved one. It is our job to provide beautiful gathering spaces for that to happen. To do that, we need set tikanga that we follow to keep us spiritually safe and the families spiritually settled and in tune. It's tikanga taken over from the marae. It's not written down. It's just practised. It's not something we could fire someone over or that someone could take a personal grievance against us over.

Tikanga around kai is an obvious example. Wherever there is a hui in any situation, there is food. It's the same at work. All the staff knows the tikanga is that we have our meeting then have something to eat afterwards. Our senior administrator Vanessa will always organise some food to follow if we are having a meeting.

New staff often ask, 'Do you guys eat every time you have a meeting?'

And yes, we always do, even if it is just two people. It is like going on the marae. There are a lot of heavy subjects being dealt with, so a lot of the talk is sacred. We say we have a tapu on us from speaking about this person's case and this sudden death, so we need to whakanoa. We release the tapu and have a kai to settle ourselves and bring us back to Te Ao Mārama.

It fulfils a physical need at the same time as it serves a spiritual purpose.

Then there's the tikanga for kai in the work fridge. Oh dear. The tikanga with that is that if you put kai in the fridge you accept that it is available for anyone to eat. I believe it's a Māori thing. Here is some kai. Help yourself. It doesn't need to be said. I love the chow mein they make at the place up the road. If I can't eat it and put the rest in the fridge, and I come back and it is gone, I get a bit hōhā but I already know the tikanga.

If it is a certain kai you put there because you have dietary conditions, you label your food. It has to be yours because you can't eat other things.

We had a new staff member who put some dumplings in the fridge. One of the old staff saw them and thought, 'Dumplings! Yum!' and started eating them.

Then the new worker went to the fridge.

'Who ate my dumplings? I got them for me and my son.'

The dumpling bandit heard and came out. 'What's the problem?'

'I'm just trying to find out who ate my dumplings.'

'Oh dear. The ones in the fridge?'

'Yeah.'

'Sorry, but I only had four. I think there's ten left.'

'My son needs more than that. At my last job, we didn't touch anyone's food if it wasn't ours.'

What made it worse was that they were special dumplings because she was gluten-free, sugar-free, vegetarian — the lot. We had to tell her that is how we are at Tipene Funerals: if you leave it around, expect it to go. I hope if any of our staff move to her old workplace they will leave the food in the fridge alone.

But we also make sure when we have a kai that there will be various dietary options, not just the old-fashioned fatty food I love. Some of the older staff find that a bit weird.

We don't sell food here because there are too many rules around that, but our families can always get a kai when they come to arrange a funeral or see a loved one. They may have spent days in the hospital, grieving, and had hardly anything to eat. The kai in our fridge is for them, too. There is bread and butter to make toast and the things you need for a cup of tea.

Another tikanga is in the dressing room, which is classed as a workspace, not a public space that anyone can go into.

When we are preparing a tūpāpaku, we may have to be a bit firm with the loved one and adjust the body to fit it in the casket. Family members may be present to help with the dressing. That is okay — it is something beautiful and ceremonial. But then we need to ask them to leave while we get the body to fit.

There is tikanga with the families we work with and tikanga with our staff. It helps bring everyone who works here together, giving us a common way of doing things despite our different backgrounds.

That doesn't go down well with a lot of families — they want to be there the whole way through. Māori and Pacific Island families, in particular, don't like this. One minute, they are there dressing their loved one; the next we are asking them to leave while we fit the body in the casket, and they want to know why they can't stay and help. If they insist, we let them, but they need to know the tikanga is that there will be fiddly things we need to do to Mum that may be a bit upsetting. So, if we have to, we tell them that her head is a bit high and we are going to have to push it back. Tikanga is that we get them out of the room for ten or fifteen minutes.

Another unwritten tikanga is that we always offer families a prayer when they leave the funeral home. Ninety per cent of the time, they say yes please. This is a whakawātea, a cleansing prayer to make sure that whatever may be lingering will go forth with the body when it departs.

During Covid, we sprayed, cleaned and sanitised everything between families — really hard out, all day, every day. The whakawātea is doing the same thing on a spiritual level.

To our new staff members, this is an awesome tikanga. If a family takes a tūpāpaku away from us to do their own tangi, the karakia is even more important. We won't be going to the church with them, so we make our own little church here. You feel better when you have the prayers. And you notice the difference when you don't.

Another staff tikanga is that every time we get a new employee, they get a proper welcome or pōwhiri. Everyone knows there is a monetary value when you employ someone. The money you are paying them will come back to you because of the quality of the work they bring to you and your business. But there is another value to our staff members — a spiritual and emotional one money can't buy. And we have a tikanga to acknowledge this.

When a new person starts, we have a gathering. Any business should do that — take the person somewhere, have a cheers and the person thinks, 'Holy moly, they have gone out of their way to welcome me.'

We are a bit more structured with our welcomes. We might (very much 'might') put on a hāngi. First, we have speeches and prayers and let them say a few words about how they feel. Then we lift the tapu by eating together.

For a lot of workplaces, this is impractical. Even for us, it can be hard to arrange if we are busy and we can't get all the staff together at the same time. Sometimes a person has been with us for a couple of weeks before we have had a chance to welcome them officially. But the welcome always happens sooner or later.

Pākehā, in particular, can get a bit overwhelmed by it. The worker I had — let's call her the dumpling lady — couldn't get her head around all this being put on just for her. A little bit was in te reo Māori and the rest was in English and we explained to her what it was about. She was blown away. It made her feel so welcome. Another benefit of this tikanga is that if you treat staff with that sort of respect, they will treat your clients with the same respect and make them feel special.

KAIORA

Tikanga is a big part of our identity at Tipene Funerals. There is tikanga with the families we work with and tikanga with our staff. It helps bring everyone who works here together, giving us a common way of doing things despite our different backgrounds.

Everyone wants to have a gathering when someone dies. They want to unite and have a ceremony for their loved one. It is our job to provide beautiful gathering spaces for that to happen.

When we have someone new, especially if they have been working at a more traditional (I probably mean 'Pākehā' when I say that) funeral home, it is a special time. We want our company to be a Māori company but also a diverse one.

That means we have people with different values and ways of doing things. We are protective of our group and the relationships we have within it, so we are picky about who we bring into the circle. We don't just say, 'This is the job, off you go.' We want to know that we can connect with them.

I went to a Pākehā business school, Manukau Institute of Technology, where we were taught very different kinds of tikanga. We weren't taught anything about pōwhiri. Maybe the equivalent is that there will be a morning tea for new staff in a Pākehā business.

If you join a Māori business, you expect a pōwhiri to welcome you. The pōwhiri is a bit more ceremonial than a morning tea. There are a few bases you have to touch on or it isn't proper.

You are not really part of Tipene Funerals until you have had a pōwhiri. It becomes very important to people.

We once had two staff start around the same time — Andrew and Mary. We had a mihi for Andrew when he started, and a kai a day later. Mary knew that someone else had had a pōwhiri as well as a kai and wanted to know why Andrew didn't get the same.

'Should we change a funeral time so we can have a kai?' I asked.

'No.'

So we changed the kai time instead — of course — and still did it so everyone could be present. Now, there are just too many people and we have adjusted the tikanga so that it doesn't require every single member of staff to be at a pōwhiri for it to be considered a proper one.

I wasn't taught at business school to feed our staff. I was taught to be good to them, but that can mean lots of different things. There are times with our staff when I know a karakia is necessary, especially if they are feeling really upset with a particular case.

Once, one of the team came back from being with a family and she was at the bottom of the stairs, almost hyperventilating and unable to move. She was able to let it out and had a tangi.

'Are you okay?' I asked. 'What is wrong? Have something to eat.'

'I just feel I've given my all but not enough.'

She had been working with a family who had lost a baby at about eight months. She witnessed Baby being embalmed, the family doing the dressing — it became a lot for her to keep inside.

'Shall we just have a karakia now?' I asked. I knew she was from a religious background.

We did and I told her I would come to the crematorium with her, that we could take Baby together. I hadn't realised till then that babies are very sensitive for her. She has lots of nephews and nieces, and she likened this baby to one of her own. It was the first time she had cared for a dead baby and that was hard for her.

So I felt a karakia was necessary and I hadn't learnt that at business school.

I did learn that sometimes you should give your staff what they call 'professional supervision', which is a form of counselling for funeral directors to help with the emotional side of the job. I hadn't heard about it till I went on a funeral directors' course. People from other funeral homes were talking about 'the first time I went on a supervision' and I didn't know what they were talking about.

'Oh, is that like having a kai together?' I asked. 'That's what we do after a funeral and that is us for the day.'

They said it was and that sounded like a good way of putting it. The difference with our tikanga is that it happens all the time and the big emotional problems don't get a chance to build up. Since then, we have issued a standing invitation to the staff to say if they need some assistance, and we can set it up, but no one has yet.

SEVEN

TANGI

Respecting different tikanga in our work means managing differences. There are Pasifika ways of doing things, Pākehā ways and Māori ways — we have to be aware of them and adjust what we do.

FRANCIS

As we have said, tikanga changes according to the situation, the environment and the immediate needs of the whānau and everyone who has gathered at that time and place.

For example, on a marae, the tikanga for a tangihanga is that we put the tūpāpaku into the wharenui and we eat in another space, in the wharekai. It is important that they are separate. But in a family house, sometimes there might be an open-plan kitchen and living room, and so you have to share the space between the kai and the tūpāpaku. Then the tikanga changes and you just have to make it work by adapting to the environment and situation.

I've taken a body to an apartment that was on the fifth floor of a building, and we had to go up in an elevator. That raises questions, like: Where do we start the karanga — down the bottom at street level or when the elevator doors open on the fifth floor?

Some people are not happy about these changes. 'This is not our tikanga.' Well, a lot of things aren't. We are having to adapt to this new modern life and the situations we are faced with. Tikanga is really about making things work. The tikanga allows us to move a bit and it can, too, while the kawa stays the same. There will always be a prayer, for instance, but it might be a different prayer.

We normally have hākari after a funeral. Now tikanga has changed because people are busy and jobs are scarce and hard to come by, so that kind of big feast may not be practical. We have the kai before instead. Have the funeral, then depart. We are changing tikanga to adapt to this new way of life. The kawa is that food will be part of a tangi; the tikanga is how and when we have the food.

Tangihanga used to last for days, as opposed to what happened at Pākehā funerals, which were really short. There is no kawa around the timeframe for tangihanga now. Technology has played a part in this. Before we had the new embalming products, the kawa was that the body would be taken and prepared with kawakawa leaves, taken onto the marae, and the first hint of odour was the signal that it was time to bury the body. That could have been from two to five days, depending on the size of the person. People were probably not as overweight then as we are now. Bodies would have been in better condition and lasted longer.

Respecting different tikanga in our work means managing differences. There are Pasifika ways of doing things, Pākehā ways and Māori ways — we have to be aware of them and adjust what we do.

In a church, the minister is in charge. On some marae, which have a strong kawa, they hand the mana of the marae over to you as a whānau if you are hiring it for a funeral. That means you can run the marae under your kawa. The initial pōwhiri and welcome is done under the kawa of their marae. Once you get given the mantle, you can run the kawa according to where you are from.

That is likelier to happen somewhere like Auckland because those attending will be a diverse group, with their home marae spread out around the country. It allows everyone to come together with a shared way of doing things for as long as the funeral lasts. Things like that are important for our survival here in the city. I don't think that would happen on a rural home marae.

Up north, we have a kawa that in a tangi the tūpāpaku always lies on the floor. That is so it can be as close as possible to Papatūānuku, Mother Earth. That never changes. At least it hasn't till lately. We are observing that a lot of old people can't get that low to hongi their loved one, which is also an important part of saying goodbye. A lot of the old people can touch the casket and say, 'Haere rā,' but you can't beat a kiss.

I have donated a couple of our chapel trolleys to the marae so that the body can be placed on them and be high enough for everyone to reach. I think that is beautiful but it also needs to be discussed and debated because it is new. Suddenly, we might be putting a trolley between the tūpāpaku and Papatūānuku.

We recently had a kuia who couldn't reach, so we picked the casket up and tilted it so she could give the tūpāpaku a kiss. How practical is that on a marae? Don't know. But, in my world, it is about getting the job done. That lady just wanted a kiss. It looked a bit silly, okay, but she got what she wanted.

We are changing tikanga to adapt to this new way of life. The kawa is that food will be part of a tangi; the tikanga is how and when we have the food.

Perhaps the casket could be put on a ramp so the head is higher but the feet are still on the ground. People are sensible. They will focus more on the destination than the road they use to get there. If there is a big change being considered, I like the fact that there will be a discussion about it. If the conclusion is that, no, we won't change it, then that is okay.

But tikanga will give way to practicalities if it's necessary. How annoyed I get personally by people not following tikanga depends on where I am. In my funeral home or any other comfort zone, I can fix it so that people know the proper way to do things.

But if we are out in public among a mass group, it can get tricky, especially if it's something I know a bit about. Once, at a marae for a tangihanga, there was a problem when it came time to put the lid on and close the coffin. You leave that as late as possible, so that if someone has a lot of mokopuna they all get a chance to see them one last time — and this lady had a lot of mokopuna.

Whenever we are putting the lid on, we always put a cloth on the face. That is a Tipene Funerals tikanga. It provides a barrier between the tūpāpaku and the coffin lid. And it needs to be in the right place or there is no point.

At this marae, up to this point, I had followed the tikanga that the wahine told me was what they did there. But then I noticed the facecloth hadn't been put on properly.

Before I could intervene and fix it, my cousin hit my hand and said, 'If you don't get in and put that cloth on, I'm going to do it.'

So I was right all along.

KAIORA

About three years ago, after the first season of our show, one of my aunties got in touch with me. She was staunch and strong. She was the person who was always there on the marae ready to give advice, or who had the information you needed. She and my uncle had decided to go back to Pawarenga to retire. She told me she wanted me to take care of things in her last days.

'Okay, Aunty. No problem.'

'No, I need you to listen.'

Oh gosh, here we go.

'I want to be cremated.'

That's a big move for someone living in Pawarenga. For some Māori, cremation goes against tikanga. Burial is a strong tradition. But she wanted to break with tradition and be cremated.

It had never been done there before, especially by someone in her generation. It would be complicated, too, because the tangi would be on the marae at Pawarenga, then she would have to be transferred to a crematorium and the closest was in Kerikeri.

I knew this wasn't going to work.

'Oh,' I said when I heard what she wanted.

'What's that supposed to mean?'

'Aunty, you know your people. They won't let me take you. I can't do that.'

'Now, whakarongo — no one else is going to do this. Only you will be allowed to do it. You and Francis are my key people and I need you to do it.'

I felt a massive sense of responsibility to get my aunty to the crematorium. Doing it was fine — but knowing that people would be fighting to stop it happening was challenging.

'This world is changing — ko te ao hurihuri tēnei,' she told me. 'There are things coming and evolving that our elderly can't keep up with.'

Often it is hard for the elderly to adapt, but she was all for the next generation. She felt the old people were too set in their ways and should allow the next generation to take over and do things their way.

Before she passed, I asked my cousin to read out a goodbye letter to her. It was just the words of a committal, which is what you use when the loved one is about to go into the furnace or the ground. I realised those words should be shared while she was alive to hear them, so she knew how much we loved her.

She sent me back a voice message — as hard as it was for her to talk — and managed to tell us how much she loved us, and that Francis and I had a lot of work to do for our people. It was very special to get that message.

Soon after, it was clear she didn't have long to go and I rushed to be there but sadly didn't get there in time.

There is only one priest for the whole of the Hokianga and he was running late. My cousins and I were stopped outside holding the casket. The kaumātua wouldn't let us go on until the priest was there. They looked at me like I should know what to do. I broke with tradition and said we should lie Aunty down on the mahau in front of this marae. There was nowhere else to go.

That was the first time we had done that and I thought that was typical of Aunty — making changes even in death. In the end, the priest showed up an hour and a half late. We had already gone into the church and had the karakia and hīmene without him and he got there just as we were coming out of the church. The urupā was just outside the church and he managed to bless the grave for her.

As it turned out, in the last two weeks before she died, Aunty changed her mind. She told her children her tūpuna had spoken to her. And she is buried in the urupā at St Gabriel's, in Pawarenga, where Francis's Pop is also in the ground.

***

This job crosses cultural boundaries all the time. On my funeral directors' course, we were given the opportunity to go on a marae. Half the class hadn't been on one before.

A couple of them said to me, 'It is amazing that you feel right at home here, Kaiora.' But I wasn't at home and I didn't feel like it. I didn't know what the tikanga was on this marae.

One of the matua gave us a rundown of the tikanga. His kōrero was a bit of a lecture to us wannabe funeral directors. He talked about what had been happening at funerals. He complained that funeral directors had been rushing. They would come in, put the body on the ground, and by the time he finished the karakia, 'You fellas have bolted.' Everyone laughed but it was serious.

Francis had come with me that day to see how the class worked. He nudged me and said, 'Does that sound like us?'

I thought it sounded like everyone there, judging from their reaction.

'In all fairness,' said the matua, 'I know you have other whānau to care for and often that is your excuse, and we know you have many tūpāpaku to care for. But hanging round for a bit of karakia makes us feel you truly care about our ways.'

In a tangi the tūpāpaku always lies on the floor. That is so it can be as close as possible to Papatūānuku, Mother Earth.

The non-Māori in my class had interesting explanations: 'Oh, we thought we would offend you if we stayed when we didn't understand what you were saying.' Some said they felt awkward because they just didn't know what to do. They weren't sure about following through until they could check the body with the lid off. In other words, they didn't know the tikanga, which meant they didn't know what to do, which meant they just gave up and left.

The matua told them a little about whakapapa. 'If you have some connection with anyone at the marae, you are safe. You have to have a connection with the tangata whenua, not the manuhiri. You should already have been several times, so then you know our process.' The course was in Wellington and he invited everyone who lived there to come back again the next day to learn more.

That's what I think a lot of Pākehā funeral directors need — a sense of connection so they know they can do things if they need to.

FRANCIS
One tribe that has a beautiful tikanga for tangi that is unique to them is Tainui — my wife's royal connection. Down there, they do funerals like everyone is royalty. Everyone dresses up in black. All the marquees are put up. Their tikanga stays the same — it doesn't move like it might in other places. That tells me that the culture is strong. Everyone knows the tikanga, so there is no need to alter it.

Tainui align themselves with the tikanga. In Auckland and other places, we bring the tikanga down to align with us. We are multi-iwi, multi-hapū and there are people who don't know anything about their culture until they come to a tangi and someone tells them about it.

In the first episode of *The Casketeers*, we had an important Tainui funeral, that of King Tūheita's sister. That just took my breath away. His blessing to permit that to be filmed set the way for every other family to think it was okay to show tangi on TV, so I am very grateful to the king for that.

The funeral didn't go to Tūrangawaewae but was on Waahi Paa, which is the royal family's own marae and a more intimate setting. Beautiful things happened. There was a lot of pomp. Part of the tikanga around kai is that you wait for the king to come in and sit down before anyone else does. I wasn't interested in the food, for once. I was just looking around, staring at the king and the people with him and what they all did.

Elsewhere, you stand when a tūpāpaku comes in, but if everyone is sitting when a priest or kaumātua arrives they stay sitting. Not if it's the king. Then you have to wait for him to leave before anyone else can leave. The people know they have to wait. They want the king to hurry up if they have finished their kai, but if he is still talking to his people there is nothing they can do about it.

Some people say it's bollocks but I think it is quite beautiful. You learn good behaviour, patience, good culture and manners from this tikanga. We don't have to go over to England to the palace to have dinner with that queen, because we have our own tikanga here for our Māori king.

The whole experience brought to light that our whānau needs to explore Kaiora's Tainui connections and the whakapapa for the kids.

EIGHT

TAPU AND NOA

Tapu is the sacred and spiritual world; noa is the profane and earthly world. In our daily lives, we go back forth between one and the other.

FRANCIS

Tapu and noa are related but different. They are like kawa and tikanga in that way. Tapu is the sacred and spiritual world; noa is the profane and earthly world. In our daily lives, we go back forth between one and the other.

They are concepts that are relevant to all aspects of life but are especially important around death and tangihanga.

At a tangihanga, the call comes from the front gate of the marae. We are in the mode of mourning and go up to kiss or hongi the body, then sit down, exchange kōrero and waiata and hongi each other.

We have gone into a realm of sacredness. The same thing happens at the funeral home — some parts are tapu and some are noa. When you come into our chapel, you know we are not in the casket area. We are in another realm.

On the marae at a tangi, people can talk about anything and everything. It's a perfect opportunity to do that because you have a ready-made audience. The kōrero doesn't have to be about the person who is dead. Actually, the occasion doesn't have to be a tangi — it could also be a wedding or a birthday.

You get politicians turning up campaigning, people turning up to say things they would never get a chance to say any other time. The wharenui fills up with kōrero over several days. And all that talk brings an element of sacredness with it, because what we say in there has been left for the walls to take in and hold. With that, we are all adorned with tapu. It is not so much sacred in a heebie-jeebie way but in terms of what is happening in there.

Sometimes, I have gone to pay respects, perhaps on the second day of a tangi, when it has been going on for a while. And as I enter that realm of tapu, I can feel it physically. It may be in the form of a little sadness, or butterflies in my stomach. You are sharing the experience with the kirimate, the mourners. That is why it is important as a mourner to go into tapu and come back to noa.

Some males get nervous at this stage, when we have to quickly gather our thoughts because we have to share some speech with those who are already there. We have to think of what we are going to say and find the right whakataukī, and there is no pen or paper. I prefer to have pen and paper because I am very forgetful. Speech-making is usually impromptu and you have to gather your thoughts quickly.

Away from the marae, at the funeral home, we have a system to uphold tapu and noa. Some people say, 'This is a funeral home, not a marae. It's very different.' But most of the time, the family want to be brought into the realm of tapu too, even though they are not on a marae. And for those of us who work here with tūpāpaku all the time, it is a marae and we feel the full heaviness of tapu.

When we have been made tapu, we need to lift that tapu in order to return to the state of noa. In the wharenui, it has been about death, sorrow and sadness. Now we want to return to the world of light. Just as we feel the tapu going in, we get the sense of noa coming out again.

When we have finished, people wash their hands, not just for hygiene but as a ritual cleansing. Then we have food to relieve us from the tapu that has been happening so that when we leave we are back in the world of the living.

It is about saying: 'Things are back to normal.' Nothing is more basic or normal than kai. But it only needs to be a little bit of food. After all, as well as the coronavirus, we have an obesity epidemic at the moment.

There are times when I take a tūpāpaku to a marae and, when I have finished, I am invited to have a kai. 'Francis, come and eat something before you go.' So I go and have nibble. Or I say, 'Thank you, I'll stop on the way up the road and grab something.'

It's usually the older generation wanting to make sure I am okay. They might think I am going to go crazy or pōrangi because of all the tapu I am taking in. If they think I am going to have something to eat to lift it, they won't worry.

When we leave the wharenui with the tūpāpaku, we are still in the realm of death. We go to the cemetery for the prayers, hymns and committal process. We still carry a burden of sacredness. And when we leave the cemetery after laying the body to rest, we wash

The wharenui fills up with
kōrero over several days.
And all that talk brings
an element of sacredness
with it, because what we
say in there has been left
for the walls to take in and
hold. With that, we are all
adorned with tapu.

our hands to relieve us of tapu from within the cemetery. It is a real sacred thing.

Then we go back to the marae and finish the kaupapa. We have some speech-making and another prayer to really lift the tapu off the immediate family and others, to transition from the world of carrying the burden of the mate, the deceased, to Te Ao Mārama.

The immediate family are a special case. They have been carrying the heaviest burden. So we need to uplift their tapu with karakia and hongi. We touch and press noses and heads to welcome the family back into the world of noa. They have been sitting there feeling they have been through the wringer, staying with the casket and going through intense grief. We are not saying the grief has finished by performing these acts. Grief goes on for as long as it takes, possibly forever. But we are moving onto a new stage.

And to seal the deal, we are going to eat. Kai is especially important now because during the time of tangihanga, the kirimate would have been cut off and not eaten with the rest of us. Now we will all eat together as things get back to normal.

Then the family becomes noa. You will notice they have a good laugh. We get them to laugh during speech-making or kai, entertain them with waiata. We hope, if they have been crying at the casket for three or four days, that now they have run out of tears — kua pau ngā roimata.

People say Māori funerals go on forever. I am one who moans and groans about how long things take. There are times when I have left tangi because work meant I had to get back to Auckland. But there are good reasons why things take so long. There is an important process that must be carried out.

I am so grateful to our ancestors who put this tikanga and kawa in place. It is definitely helpful with processing grief. We don't just bury the body and say it is all over. We go through a rather arduous process to drain us of tears. It is a communal counselling session to help everyone pass through it.

And it is very open. Generally crying is done in private behind glasses and hankies. This is so open.

There are many different forms of being able to pay your respects. Haka is another way to express aroha and grief openly. As are speech and waiata.

Very occasionally, respecting tapu can still be at odds with the modern world. I was called to a case where someone had dropped dead in a shopping mall. Naturally, everyone was taken by surprise and it took a while to work out what to do.

It was a Māori family and they wanted a karakia before the body was taken away. The police and medics should have picked that body up and put it in an ambulance or moved it somewhere out of the way. Instead, the body was left in the middle of the mall, covered with a blanket.

I was called and shot over there quickly. I backed up to the door and walked in carrying my stretcher. Once I got inside, the police wanted me to remove the body straight away and to do a karakia later. If the police had already moved the body to a discreet space, there wouldn't have been the pressure there was when I got arrived. That's not even tikanga. That's common sense.

But I performed the karakia to help the family be at peace, because that is what they wanted and needed.

The family were focused on the tapu of the event. They didn't care about where they were or who was walking past. They were sad and they needed a prayer. So we had a prayer and a hīmene in the middle of the mall, and after that I took the body and the family went away.

That was actually an eye-opener for me. I understood that what mattered most for them was knowing their loved one's spirit would be okay.

Knowing their loved one's spirit would have heard something in their language, right there in the mall, relieved their wairua and settled their spirit. That was an important lesson in my career. I understood the importance of karakia — whether in a mall or a hospital or a house — to help us move the spirit on.

In the end, waiting for us to have the karakia first helped the police to do their job and to get the information they needed. Otherwise, the family would have been too agitated. They got their report done much faster by having the karakia, and along the way I understood more about my culture.

If it had been a Pākehā case, I think the family would have reacted differently. 'I'm not looking at the body. Take it away.'

Naturally, all the people around knew something was up. I registered that they were walking past quickly. But for the whānau and me, we were in the moment. We didn't really notice them.

* * *

About twenty years ago, the word tapu was used only in special cases — usually around death and to talk about areas we don't go to. 'Don't do this — it is tapu.' Or 'Don't go there — it is tapu.' But we didn't use the word that often.

Back then, it was absolutely sacred. Just thinking about it gave you the heebie-jeebies. You didn't muck around with it. Even gang members, when they came into cemeteries, for instance, would know the word and observe the rituals around it.

But there was a downside. People avoided cemeteries, so they were being neglected because they were too tapu. 'I'm not going to mow the lawn, it's too tapu.' Or 'I'm not going to wash the grave, it's too tapu.'

Now we are more relaxed about things — as long as we adhere to the tikanga of the place — and the word is used more widely. For example, in our home I might say, 'Don't go to that area, it is out of bounds — He tapu tēnei wāhi mo tēnei wā.' Back then, I would not have used the word tapu. I would have just said don't go there.

I use the word frequently. I might say my office is a sacred space and put a rāhui on it to tell people they are not welcome there between ten and twelve. Once, I would have said it was out of bounds. Now I say it is tapu. Not that there is anything holy about it, but it is a good way to express that I seriously want people to stay away for those two hours, so I can get my work done without being disturbed.

Which things are defined as tapu or noa changes, but they do tell people how to behave. I might use them in a relaxed tone but their meanings are not casual. So if I say my office is tapu, everyone knows I mean it.

Our kaumātua are encouraging us to make tapu part of our lives in a way that is a bit less formal. They know if they continued on the path of being very serious and using it to scare people, a whole generation might have given up on our tikanga and our

In the wharenui, it has been about death, sorrow and sadness. Now we want to return to the world of light. Just as we feel the tapu going in, we get the sense of noa coming out again.

way of culture, because it was just too much. They want them to understand the word is sacred and we mean it, but to also use it more often and make sacredness part of our view of the world we live in.

Pākehā don't use the words tapu and noa but they show the same attitudes in different ways. For instance, a Pākehā funeral home has a reception lounge for food. They don't eat in their chapel. Their chapel is tapu. And food is for later in another place. They may not say their kai is about the noa, but they still use it to mark the end of the tangi and a transition back to normal life.

One's home is tapu to the people who live there. It is a sacred place and there is tikanga for that. We had karakia when we moved into the house we are living in at the moment. We didn't know what happened prior to us coming here and we wanted to bless the house.

We had whānau and non-whānau telling us there was a gentleman ghost here — a lovely man who smiled at them. There were moments we felt there might have been someone there too, so we had karakia for him. We weren't trying to shoo him on, because only beautiful things prevail in this house. We don't mind him being here. He might be the builder or an original matua or tupuna. If we have a ghost, that's kei te pai. It doesn't really bother us. It might bother me if I saw it, but I haven't. I have only heard a few things that aren't right. We can share the space if we establish a relationship.

The ghost also might be here because we are two doors from a cemetery, which I really love. If I ever own my own home, I want it to be near a cemetery, because it is so beautiful and powerful.

Our location means we walk or drive by the cemetery every day, so we may be crossing paths with the spirits. They may be going through the house on their way to the water. And they are welcome, as long as they don't upset us but only do lovely things and are just stopping here to say hello.

This is a tapu, so we have prayer to protect the family and we ask for a guiding hand from a power higher than us. We protect our home. At work, we bless everything new, such as the cars and equipment we will use when we are working with the mate. Even when we sell our funeral cars, we bless them with a little karakia because we want the new owners to enjoy them as much as we did.

KAIORA

My father taught us about tapu and noa in the home. Although he loved laying down the law for other people about whakapapa and other matters, I don't think he tried to instruct them on tapu and noa.

His version of tapu was focused on things like not allowing any hair on the table. Certain parts of the body were tapu. Your head is tapu. You don't just sit at a table and brush your hair. You can't sit on something if you eat off it. Tapu and noa are about keeping things separate. You won't have respect for anything if there is no tapu.

I instil the same things in my children, although more with actions than with words. They know not to sit on the table, or to brush their hair at the table, or to put haircare products on the table. Because the table is for food, which is noa, and anything to do with the head is tapu.

In my work, with my experience around tūpāpaku, I am very aware that their body has become tapu. This has come down from my father's teaching. They have lived a life and I have to treat them as sacred. So when I wash and dry them, I do it carefully and with feeling and a karakia.

This is a case where I wish I knew more. I'm happy to admit that and for people to know that I don't know everything. My love for tikanga doesn't make me an expert — I'm just someone trying to live my life in the right way. In some cases, I might know the rules but not know why they are there. I have uncles I can ask, but they all have their own varying perspectives. And I have read works by scholars, like Māori Marsden and Ranginui Walker, but find my personal experiences with tapu and noa can be different.

NINE

MANAAKITANGA

There is nearly always an opportunity to practise manaakitanga, no matter where you are or what you are doing — and remember, it uplifts you as well as the person you are caring for.

FRANCIS

People use the word manaakitanga to mean hospitality, but there is more to it than that.

If you look at the word, you have 'mana' and 'aki' and 'tanga'. Most of us know what mana is: 'Oh man, the All Blacks, when they do the haka, I feel the mana.' That is a beautiful perspective.

'Aki' is to lift and build someone up by encouraging and supporting them. Lifting their mana up. And 'tanga' is the doing — the '-ing' on the end of a word in English.

The extra component is what comes back to you. Because if you do it properly and extend manaakitanga to someone the right way, you build yourself up as well.

When you feed someone, you build them up by making sure they are comfortable. But at the same time, you are getting something back. You are increasing your mana, adding to your reputation as someone who is good at caring for people. It is a two-way street if done correctly.

Manaakitanga and kaitiakitanga, or guardianship, are very close, especially when practised in the home. At home, I am the kaitiaki — I look after and treasure and take care of my children. I feed them and hopefully teach them good foundations for life, with lessons they can take when they go out into the world on their own. That is how we manaaki our children. It is holistic.

In fact, manaakitanga starts at home. It's no good being the super-host and taking care of everyone else if your own home is not in order.

Because of that, manaakitanga is very much an everyday thing. It is not just a special occasion thing. You don't just practise it when you have guests. It must be ingrained and extended everywhere you go.

Outside of the whānau, manaakitanga is definitely about being hospitable. If you reduce it to its simplest form, it is about being caring and mindful. That is the true way. In being caring and mindful, we are building someone's mana up.

On the marae and in the wharenui, the pōwhiri process is a form of manaakitanga. The main point of a pōwhiri is to connect people with each other.

A lot of Pākehā might think it is daunting going on the marae, with the wero, the taiaha, the hongi. It can be daunting for people. They might rather watch it on TV than practise it. But when it is being extended to you, it is actually manaakitanga that is occurring, whether you are Pākehā or Māori.

It gives the home people of the marae the opportunity to greet you in a formal manner. They don't want you to stumble on in unprepared. They want to welcome you officially so they can make you feel comfortable. It shows they do care about you. This is a huge part of Māori culture.

On the taumata, people get ready for the manuhiri. They have a look to see who is coming. 'Oh, there is so-and-so from that marae.' If they know some people in your group, they will point them out because they want to make the speeches relatable. The speaker doesn't do this to make himself sound amazing — even if it does — but to make sure his manaakitanga is the best it can be.

If the people are from Mt Eden, over the hill, he will say, 'All you people from Mt Eden — welcome to those of you from under our beloved mountain standing proud in the middle of Auckland.' They even build the maunga up.

So even with speech-making, which has so many aspects we talk about elsewhere in this book, everything comes down to manaakitanga.

It is such a big, important word — Māori people don't really use it because it is just in the culture to do it. It's like not talking about breathing, it is so basic.

It underlies so much of Māori tradition that is being incorporated into all sorts of events that aren't particularly Māori in themselves. When we are opening a building in the middle of town, or a new park, the fact that someone will be there to kōrero is about manaakitanga. Yes, keeping Treaty of Waitangi obligations is part of it, but at the end of the day it is asking for the grace of God on the wharenui or the park. It does not just occur on the marae platform. It is appropriate wherever we are, just as we had a karakia at our new house. We stand there and do it wherever we are with a karakia and a mihi to acknowledge our

Manaakitanga is very much an everyday thing. It is not just a special occasion thing. You don't just practise it when you have guests. It must be ingrained and extended everywhere you go.

new surroundings and the builders who made them and ask for God's grace to be upon it all. We will take tikanga Māori wherever we need to.

* * *

Most of my examples of manaakitanga are funeral-related, but I often think back to how much of a part it played in my early life with the love of my Nan and Pop.

Once again, they didn't teach us manaakitanga, they lived it. Every time we went to town to get something they would overbuy, and end up overcooking, because they never knew who would turn up and be hungry, and they could not bear the idea of not being able to manaaki someone by feeding them. I'm sure that was part of their upbringing, too.

I would like to have known more about their early lives, but they didn't speak about them a lot. One of the blessings for me and my wife is that we have a written record of a few things in our life. I am glad my own children will know a little about their background from the books we have written.

Our parents love us, help us learn, and look after us. For me, it was Nan and Pop who raised me; for my wife, it was her mum and dad. They give us so much to help us at the start of life.

Then when they get older, we think about them differently. Our form of manaakitanga is to stay with them and look after them, but so many Pākehā send them to rest homes. And here is where Pākehā and Māori could maybe learn more from each other. A lot of Māori or Pacific Island people say they couldn't let their old people live in rest homes. But retirement villages are so beautiful nowadays — I see a lot of them in my work, so I know. In my heart and mind, when we send Nan or Pop to a retirement village, I think that is one of the best things we can do as manaakitanga.

We are born and they look after us, and we need to figure out a way to say thank you to Nan and Pop. The last thing we can do before they leave the world is show them manaakitanga in their final days. I would love to see Nan living in a retirement village because I know she would get better care there. Not many whānau can give their old people the same level of care that professionals can.

I have to acknowledge, though, that there is another side to this. Some of the care places aren't very well run. The more money you have, the better they get looked after.

Generally, it's not a one-size-fits-all thing. Everyone thinks it would be lovely for old people to stay with their whānau till they pass away. But often when families try to do that, it isn't lovely for anyone. The old people are not looked after properly. The whānau resent it.

I like the way Pākehā manaaki their elders. I like the way we do it, too, but Māori and Pacific Island people are going to retirement homes now and it can mean they get proper care.

As far as our own children are concerned, I think growing up around the funeral business will give them a good grounding in manaakitanga. They see their parents being thoughtful and kind to so many people and they just assume that that is how people are supposed to behave. They don't think it's a job.

When our sons Nikora and Moronai come to the funeral home after school, they take their hats off as soon as they come in. They don't speak above a whisper and they go straight upstairs where our offices are and stay out of the way, even if there is no one in the building for a funeral. If they are eating something, they close the door so the smell won't waft downstairs. They check whether there are any families in the building before they go anywhere. We have come close to driving home without them sometimes because they are so quiet.

I once heard someone ask one of the boys to direct them to the toilet. 'Follow me,' he said. 'I will take you there.' We didn't have to tell him to do it. I was so happy because he was showing me I can trust him to do things. He knows what is right.

Just as you can build your own tikanga at home, so you can develop your own manaakitanga as something you want your children to grow up in. We don't say the word so much, because it is an action. It is practised more than it is spoken of.

Our boys are still normal kids, of course. They fight between each other like any siblings. But they know to share. When their cousins visit, they take them to their rooms to play with their toys. They don't need us to tell them to practise manaakitanga. And then the adults can have something to eat and drink and have a conversation.

Nikora is fifteen now and that's supposed to be a bad teenage time. But it doesn't have to be like that. The other day, we had his aunty and uncle over. He came out and said, 'Hi Aunty, hi Uncle,' and gave them a kiss and hug. I thought, 'Good — it's working!' That is the fruits of the labour my wife and I have been doing.

The lessons they learn at the funeral home are good ones to take to other places. They are not just about what to do when someone has lost a loved one. They teach you how easy it is to be nice to people in general and to make them feel good.

Everyone can practise it and in their own way. It's all good, as long as you are uplifting someone. There is enough going on in this world that puts people down.

During the Covid lockdowns, our prime minister asked us all to be kind. If our Māori MPs were onto their game, they would have given that phrase to the prime minister as, 'Ngā manaakitanga — please show manaakitanga.' It would have brought the word out a bit more.

As with so many other concepts we are talking about, Pākehā do the same thing and get the same results from it — it's just talked about in a slightly different way. In Māori culture, the manaakitanga concept emphasises the balance between what each side gets out of it more than Pākehā culture does. But Māori or non-Māori, we are very hospitable people who look after one another. Our prime minister reflects it in the way she represents us to the world and the world has noticed.

KAIORA
I have realised while working on this book that every time I get a term to think about, even if it is something I might use or mention every day without much thought, it is actually something really big. Manaakitanga is no exception. It is a huge part of what we do, as funeral directors, employers, parents, whānau and friends — every aspect of life. It's something we can't block. It is part of who we are. It is in our job description for all our endeavours.

For me, manaakitanga is quite a lot more than 'hospitality'. It is closest in meaning to tiaki, or caring. They are the same sort of values.

Within a family, it is important to practise manaakitanga between all the members. The family is a framework through which it should always be applied, with everyone looking out for everyone else.

For me, it all began in the whānau with my siblings, and with whanaungatanga, which is usually translated as the kind of relationship you get from sharing experiences together — so it can refer to blood relations but also to other kinds of relationship.

My older siblings might have a different understanding of how this worked. They got beatings here and there as a way of teaching them how to behave.

But I was the cheeky younger sister who got away with pretty much everything. My dad was very staunch about the older ones looking after the younger ones, the tuakana–teina dynamic.

As a teina, you naturally look up to the elder siblings for advice, and as a tuakana, you expect your younger siblings to have your back, so it is vice versa. You don't have to be blood-related. It can be a relationship between siblings, but it can also be any other kind of pair where the older one can teach or manaaki the younger. If someone is a senior member of your profession, you might consider them a tuakana. In this sense, I would say that Francis is my tuakana. Maybe.

Fehi joined our company after he had been funeral directing for two years. And Fiona has been in the profession for twenty years, so she is the tuakana to Fehi, in the sense that he needs to go to her for advice.

In my whānau framework, my siblings have always been examples for us and also been advisers on anything manaaki or tiaki. They were there when Mum and Dad weren't. There were four years when our parents weren't around much because Mum was taking Dad back and forth to Whangārei Hospital. So yes, my elder siblings were my tuakana who I had to turn to for advice and support.

I feel sorry for my boys when Nikora, who is the eldest, has to be in charge, because I remember what it was like with my elder siblings. They were mean to me when they could get away with it. You weren't so much younger brother or sister as you were a little slave. 'Go and get the feijoas.' 'Get me a drink.' I would stay out for hours just so I didn't need to go home. Then I would start playing with my mates and finally collect some feijoas and then go home. It wasn't great, but you also knew when push came to shove that they would support you because they were whānau.

* * *

Sometimes we have walk-ins at the funeral home, and they really want to talk about what they are going through. So I want to manaaki them. If I have the time, I will — and if I don't, I will still try to. 'Okay, cool. I don't want to rush you, but I have half an hour till the next client I have to see. I can talk to you after that.'

It's so automatic. I always compare it to the cup-of-tea experience. When someone comes into your home, you give them a cuppa without asking. You don't think about it. You give them whatever you can.

Well, usually. When I go into an arrangement room with someone, my staff will notice if I've forgotten to offer a cup of tea. They knock and say, 'Excuse me, would you like a cup of tea?'

Manaakitanga is an action, practised more than it is talked about. It is a huge part of what we do, as funeral directors, employers, parents, whānau and friends — every aspect of life.

And they give me a look like: 'How come you didn't? That's not like you, girl.'

There is nearly always an opportunity to practise manaakitanga, no matter where you are or what you are doing — and remember, it uplifts you as well as the person you are caring for.

When you know there is a need, you should act on it. I always feel helpless if I can't do anything. So, if you see people standing around, go and get more chairs. If there are no more chairs, then you should stand with them to show you are sharing that experience. If you don't have the thing that's missing, at least offer a substitute. If you have run out of tea, how about a glass of water? That lets the people know you are trying to do the right thing.

It really is the case that it is the thought that counts. Our staff know not to park in the very few parking spaces at the funeral home. They are strictly for customers. Once, we were taking a colleague to our car and he couldn't understand why we had to walk so far when there were empty parking spaces in front of the building.

'You should know, bro. We have to leave the space for everyone,' Francis told him. 'If people want to use our services, or drop things off, they are just here for a short time, and they should be able to park where it's handy.'

For us, the customers are the priority. He couldn't believe it.

If you think like that about small things, you will be more likely to do right when it comes to big things. Small acts of kindness are just as important as big ones. Manaakitanga can be as small as getting a chair or a glass of water, or as big as looking after someone's child if they are unable to do it themselves.

I have to admit, it can take a toll. Sometimes I get frustrated with Francis. It's like he thinks we have an endless pot of kindness that he can keep dipping into, to the point where he is exhausted and he doesn't know it. It chews away at him until it pops. You have to manaaki yourself as well as other people.

TEN

KAITIAKITANGA

We are guardians for a short time, but while we are here we also have a responsibility and need to be good examples to the next generation.

KAIORA

What stands out in kaitiakitanga is the word 'tiaki' — meaning to care for something and to care about it, too. Kaitiaki means you are the caregiver. For me, these are very basic principles and values. My dad always used that word when educating us about the land. We had our own family whenua but it didn't end there.

'You need to treat the whenua like your own land, wherever you are,' he told us. He didn't like rubbish on the ground. And he didn't like seeing waste. At home, he made us empty all the scraps into a bucket for the pigs. If there were no pigs — which there weren't after we moved to Kaitāia — we had to throw the scraps into the compost.

He didn't like seeing kai and rubbish mixed up together. I always notice it in the mall — people empty all their stuff straight into one bin. That is kai being wasted that the pigs could have.

Mainly it was about caring for the land. It's connected to the

Treaty and people's rights and duties. Guardianship is part of what's in the Treaty. A lot of artists sing about that. Stan Walker is one. All these things come to mind when people say the word kaitiakitanga.

With our own kids, looking after their toys is a good place to start learning about kaitiakitanga and the most important aspect: if you don't look after what you have been given to care for, you could lose it forever. They have so many toys; if they leave them lying around, I will hide them or put them in the rubbish. That encourages them to respect their environment. If they look after their things now, they will look after the big things when they grow up.

They need to appreciate their taonga. I like to ensure they look after their taonga. The whenua is a taonga. Our vehicles are taonga. Our whare is a taonga. I would like to ensure they know how to tiaki those.

Mihaka can't have a toy for a week without ripping it apart. Nikora, who is older, has learnt that lesson. He knows to take care of anything he has because it will be a long time before he gets another one once it's broken.

FRANCIS

The word kaitiakitanga to my mind includes an element of ownership, but also the idea that a lot of the things we think we own, we don't really. We are just kaitiaki of the whenua, looking after it while we are here. I was brought up to believe the Treaty is important, and so protests were a normal part of life. Kaitiaki seem to be involved in protests quite a lot.

When we had 1080 poison being used to control pests up around the Pawarenga area, this came up a lot. There was a lot of division and, for the kaitiaki, a lot of discussions about it.

The whenua is a taonga.
Our vehicles are taonga.
Our whare is a taonga.
I would like to ensure
our children know how
to tiaki those.

We started early. As children at school, we were bussed to hui to listen to the arguments. It was so boring. It might not seem like a good way to encourage kids to take an interest in kaitiakitanga but, even though I hated it at the time, something sank in that has helped me understand what it means to be kaitiaki. And even to form my own opinion about using 1080 — I don't want to get too political about it here, but looking at aerial photos of before and after, showing the damage possums did to the bush, made me think sometimes harsh things are necessary to get a job done. Kaitiakitanga is a balancing act.

Meanwhile, it saddens me when whānau do not get up to the whenua and clear the land and do the jobs that need to be done. I'm not an obsessive lawn-mower but, if that was my land, I would be doing things. If your whenua is in the country and covered in tea tree, you should be the kaitiaki and foster what is there. Whānau with whenua by the road or the sea have so many opportunities to make something beautiful.

This philosophy is there in the work I do, for instance, when I think about graves. When I help people choose a plot, I am like a real estate agent selling tiny sections. I take the whānau along the rows: 'Here is Section B with a view of the Waitākere Ranges. Over here is the chapel view.'

When the whānau decide on a plot for their loved one, it is important to reinforce that their tūpāpaku is kaitiaki of that plot for a certain number of years. They have to understand that. We talk about kaitiakitanga as a people, but at the same time everyone in a whānau is guardian of this small bit of land for a certain period. And that comes with responsibility. Whānau are not allowed certain flowers or fences on their plot. They have to keep them clean. These are rules to protect things for the next generation, because in time that grave, hopefully, will be used for someone else.

For now, you are the kaitiaki. I think it is important to use this word more freely and give it an explanation and meaning. My generation is very interested in ownership — even personally, when wondering whether we will ever own a house. That is ka pai but, like everyone else, we are all going to be dead one day. So even if we buy some whenua and get an architect to design a house and build it and live in it for years and raise our family in it, we are still just a guardian. Our kids will take it over and sell it after we have spent the money and paid the mortgage off.

We are guardians for a short time, but while we are here we also have a responsibility and need to be good examples to the next generation.

The time is coming in New Zealand when we will have to think about whether we still want to take up land to bury our loved ones in or think of other ways to dispose of them. That means not just cremation but also liquefying and other methods we may not have thought of yet.

With our kids, just as it did with me, it starts with what is in their daily life, like the recycling bin. We didn't have that big rubbish problem up north, because we didn't have all the things that make rubbish when we were growing up. But we do in Auckland. And it does all start at home. The way you make them behave now is the foundation of how they will be when they grow up.

Ultimately, the concept at the root of it all is that we are not here for very long, and who knows this better than a funeral director?

If your whenua is in the country and covered in tea tree, you should be the kaitiaki and foster what is there. Whānau with whenua by the road or the sea have so many opportunities to make something beautiful.

ELEVEN

MANA

Doing the haka doesn't give you mana.
You have to have mana to do the haka.

FRANCIS

For me, the best way to describe mana is to talk about how it works in my life. It is usually translated as meaning authority or reputation. Sometimes it takes the form of influence, and that can be good, or it can be used to coerce people.

The Māori culture is very verbal. There is a lot of talking. People sometimes say: too much hui, not enough doey. But that can be how mana is expressed. When you sit there listening to someone with mana, you are uplifted, spiritually and emotionally. It's the whole package.

When you watch the All Blacks do the haka, there is a lot of mana there. But doing the haka doesn't give you mana. You have to have mana to do the haka.

In the home, mana is really about integrity. If I say I am going to do something, then I will do it. This is where I show mana to the children. We want them to have mana but to use it humbly and understand what is important.

Even parking can be an issue of mana, as well as of manaakitanga. For example, one day, we went to a function and there was a lot of parking out the front. My son wanted us to park there.

'Oh, no,' I said, 'leave it for the old people.'

'Dad, no, you are allowed to park there.'

Instead, we had a long walk from the car, and I explained that putting others first and caring for them has a lot of mana. Mana doesn't mean being at the front. My son and I needed to have that conversation.

'There might be people coming with babies,' I said.

'We have a baby.'

Good point. 'But we have a pram. They may not.'

Mana does not need to be displayed. It is about kindness and thoughtfulness, as well as about authority and a display of strength.

Of course, it is associated with leadership and prominent people and authority. But all our leaders would have been at home at some point. If we are going to create great leaders and people, we need to start when they are children. A lot of kids have a lot of mana. As well as practising it in our home, the kids learn about how it works at school.

'Oh, Dad, today I did show and tell,' said Mihaka, one day after school. 'The teacher said I had a lot of mana to stand up in front of everyone and talk.'

He was on top of the world because, although he is loud at home, he is shy in public. I knew what it would have been like for him to stand up in class and show his photos of Pawarenga and Nan. So the word mana is not only for MPs and kaumātua and other important people. If our tamariki do something great, you can say, 'What great mana you have.'

Of course, there can be mana in status, like the kaumātua on the marae have. Everything is always run past them. But sometimes we may not like that kaumātua. They were young once, and people might remember: 'Oh, he was a drinker and swore and bashed the women back then, and now he is telling us what to do on the marae.'

There is a lot of that. But the status he has on the marae is about control and authority. We have to give him mana because of the role, not so much because of the person he is.

In the case of our King Tūheitia, although we may not know a lot about him as a man, he has status from his past and his tūpuna. We respect him for this. So, as well as its own qualities, mana also can come from context. This is the mana someone is born into when they come direct from our atua, born so pure and clean. If only we could be a baby again and earn mana as we grow.

There are wonderful examples of people born with mana. But there are others who have been pushed to the top, such as the late Dame Whina Cooper. She didn't want to be a leader, but she walked the walk and grabbed everyone's attention. This was a woman with so much mana. She pushed through in a man's world and a Pākehā world and got to the top. I see another clear example of true mana with our prime minister, Jacinda Ardern, and how she conducts herself.

This book is about everyday tikanga and making it usable and user-friendly at home. That extends to mana. We want our tamariki to know their mums and dads have a lot of mana. They need to understand that what someone does has mana when they are providing for others. Whether they are a lawyer or doctor or work at The Warehouse, what they do has mana because it is being done for a good reason — to provide for a family.

So there are aspects that can be taught and should be taught: to be kind, to show respect, to speak up if something is wrong.

* * *

At tangihanga, mana is manifested through waiata, kōrero, haka, the sound of the karanga: 'We have come to pay our respects to a great tree fallen in the forest of Tāne Mahuta.' What a great way to metaphorically say this man had a lot of mana, by comparing him to the great tree. That is an example of how karanga works.

Another example is when in the karanga the person says, 'We have come to pay our respects and may you be reunited with your great ancestors ...' and they mention some influential names. That gets you thinking about the person coming in. People doing a big haka or if big groups come are other ways in which mana is displayed.

At some funerals, there may not be a haka, even though the person had a lot of mana. That might not have been their wish.

In South Auckland, ordinary people and their whānau are so emotional and the person meant so much to them that they will often do the haka. Or you get big-scale tangihanga up at Bastion Point. Everyone there has a lot of mana. No matter what time I arrive, they are all out there, welcoming the tūpāpaku. This is a true iwi. That is who they are. They don't do it to showboat —

We want our tamariki to know their mums and dads have a lot of mana. They need to understand that what someone does has mana when they are providing for others.

if you ever want to feel moved, go there. The Ngāti Whātua o Ōrākei have so much mana and I am always proud to go up there.

Objects can also have mana. A greenstone taonga or a watch, for example, might be whānau heirlooms. They might have got their mana from being blessed and consecrated by a tohunga for a certain purpose. Or there might be something my grandfather owned that has come down to me.

These are treated like people, with respect for the mana they have. We do not necessarily have a ceremony to say this taonga has mana, but in your family you will know and you will want to protect it. It is hard to explain the word mana in English because it includes things like this.

Pictures and portraits are another case where mana can be relevant. There is nothing quite like this in Pākehā culture. For instance, we have the funeral ceremony called kawe mate, when you take a photo of the loved one back onto the marae, but perhaps not with the tūpāpaku. You might have had a tangi but not taken the body back to its rightful marae or to a marae that it can whakapapa to.

If I died and Kaiora took me not to my marae in Pawarenga but to her marae in Awanui, and I got buried near her dad (if I should ever be so lucky), the Pawarenga people would not be happy.

So, we would have a kawe mate, where we take the person's spirit via a photo onto the marae. Kaiora would stand at the gate with a photo of me, then call it on and take it on like a tangi. It would be placed at the front of the people and there would be speech-making, just like a funeral, but said to the photo. That photo has mana.

When my Nan said a photo of Pop couldn't go where it would be looking in the direction of the food, that was not only because of the tapu but also because of the mana of the photo.

There was a time I used to question this. I thought it was bollocks. Then someone pointed out to me what happens when we look at a photo. You see the smile, and the eyes. It brings back memories of the good times and the bad times, the relationship and experiences you shared. Photos have a lot of mana for that reason. It was a great lesson to learn.

KAIORA

To me, mana means strength and power. In recent days, every time I hear the word, I think of the Mana Party and their example of mana. Their leader, Uncle Hone Harawira, has always been an example of someone who uses his mana well.

As I understand it, mana has got to be there in you. You have to be born with it. Actually, every individual has mana, but we each have different ways of exercising it.

I've been taught mana has a whakapapa and that it comes from the gods. There is a song called 'He mana tuku iho' about goddesses: Papatūānuku, then her daughters. It tells about each one's powers. I think of them when someone talks about mana wāhine. I see this in so many women and how they hold themselves in public.

I feel it's something that can't be just taught or told. You have to experience it. And you have to be careful how you use it. Aggression is not mana.

My brothers felt they were entitled to be authoritative. When Dad passed, they felt they were the men of the whānau and had the right to lead the whānau.

'Okay, Dad has passed away, so I suppose he taught them to be like this,' I thought. I don't feel they trampled on our mana but when it came to certain things, attending certain events, for example, they felt they had the obligation to be the mouthpieces. That is a tāne thing when you go on the marae.

But it didn't stop there. We would get home and they would be trying to tell us what to do every day. I was confused. Who was actually the boss of the whānau? Them or our mum? Our dad taught us that the men's responsibility was to lead the whānau in some ways, but they took it to mean leading the whānau all the time.

When I brought Francis home to be introduced to my whānau, my brothers were hostile because he was from Pawarenga and there was some history there. 'You're not bringing your Pawarenga ways here,' they told him.

'Are you trying to exercise mana? Is this your way of doing it?' I asked. You could say it was a misuse but I think it was just typical brothers being brothers.

I have been taught mana in many different ways. For my dad, giving a blessing to someone at a house or having karakia was his way of exercising mana. There might already be a priest on a marae having karakia, but he would have a karakia, too.

He and his sister always argued about religion. She was Māori Anglican and he chose to be Mormon, and they would Bible-bash each other.

'You've got no mana,' she told him. 'You think your church has it. Doubt it.'

But I think he used his mana well. There are other people I think use their mana properly. Dame Naida Glavish is one I have so much respect for. Uncle Hone Harawira. Jacinda Ardern. Mihi

Forbes. Annabelle Lee-Mather. People who have made changes for Māori culture in the mainstream.

We see a lot of dignitaries coming through the funeral home. You think just because they are cabinet ministers or hold other high positions, they have mana. No. They have status. But sometimes you can't see any mana in them.

If mana was the same as status, you could easily lose it: if you lost the job or didn't do it properly, you could fritter away the gift of mana you had been given to start with.

It is hard in some ways for Francis and me. Because we are owners of a business, we are looked at as leaders who should have certain qualities. I feel it is difficult to live up to those standards. You can put on a performance or just be yourself. I like to go out and be myself. He will query me sometimes, 'You're wearing that today?'

'Yes, I am. Just because I don't wear a suit doesn't mean I don't have my leadership qualities on.'

Modesty is part of mana. You can sense it even in humble and quiet people. And you will be more loved when you show humility. Though I love my Uncle Hone, too.

Tamariki can definitely have mana and I see it all in my boys. They are not shy. There is no room for shyness in mana, in my view. Some shy people may have mana, but I need to see it to know it is there.

Pākehā sometimes use the word mana to describe other things, maybe because they don't have English words for the concepts they are talking about. They may get the wrong idea from the media, for instance, about the difference between authority and mana. But I love that people are using the term more in everyday conversation.

Modesty is part of mana. You can sense it even in humble and quiet people. And you will be more loved when you show humility.

TWELVE

HONGI

As soon as everything touches, we breathe in together. We close our eyes. Then we lean back and say 'kia ora'. That can be before or after. It means you are no longer visitors. We are one people.

FRANCIS

There is a famous saying: 'Tihei mauri ora.' It gets translated many ways. Sometimes, the idea of a sneeze is in there, but it always means 'the breath of life'. It is used on the marae to get people's attention at the start of a speech.

A hongi is similar — it is the act of sharing the breath of life with someone. There is a connection.

When we call visitors onto the marae, there is the pōwhiri process: visitors come on, sit and converse. You might hongi first, depending on the kawa of the area. Or it may be after the speeches that we will seal the deal with the hongi. It is much like a handshake in other settings. Shaking hands joins people together physically. We do that when we hongi and we put our nose to the other person's nose and make sure our foreheads — where our brain and thoughts are — touch as well.

Then we are going to have a hongi. And when we hongi, we breathe in together. It is not a race. We don't say, 'One, two, three, go.' As soon as everything touches, we breathe in together. We close our eyes. Then we lean back and say 'kia ora'. That can be before or after. It means you are no longer visitors. We are one people. We have shared a breath through the nose. We have shared thoughts. It's all symbolic and it's a beautiful way to connect with one another. It's a beautiful thing to be able to get intimate like that.

To non-Māori, it can be a bit much getting hard out into someone's space like that. I've hongied a few Pākehā people and they say, 'Oh, my nose is so sore.' Maybe. When you grow up with it, your nose gets used to it.

It's just a touch. We don't push noses like two bulls having a fight. I've heard some orators saying, 'Now we are going to press noses.' It is not even pressing. Then it is on to the next person. I love what it means.

A lot of people don't want to do it, and they are not forced to. If they are uncomfortable, they are uncomfortable. But the hongi and what it signifies is so beautiful. When you walk on the street or through the mall and see someone and have a hongi, a lot of people stare. But the more we do it the more normal it is.

When we hongi Pākehā people, we shouldn't make out as if they know what it's about. It's not about having a smell. We should have a little kōrero first to explain about sharing one breath and one mind and how we are unified when we do that.

Covid-19 changed that a bit. People are even more wary now, especially the elderly. When we took a tūpāpaku to a marae during the pandemic, as we went around for the hongi and harirū, those

Shaking hands joins people together physically. We do that when we hongi and we put our nose to the other person's nose and make sure our foreheads — where our brain and thoughts are — touch as well.

with respiratory conditions just bowed, so you knew not to hongi or kiss them.

There is other tikanga around tūpāpaku and the hongi. Up north, with our dead in the casket, we are supposed to get down to hongi them.

I need to think about that. They are dead, so we can't actually share a breath. Down the line, at Gisborne and Tairāwhiti, they don't touch the body. They just look at it. I think that tikanga is good. They are dead. They are a shell. There is no point to having a hongi with them. They can't do anything in return.

We need to nip all this social kissing in the bud and get back to the hongi. Kissing isn't very Māori, but on marae it's become normal now to kiss ladies and hongi men. I think it's unfair. It's like saying the ladies are not Māori but the men are. The kiss is not part of who we are.

I now make every effort to hongi a female in that setting. On the street, a kiss is okay, but on the marae we have to go back to what the hongi is about — connecting together through the nose and mind. That is more in line with kawa.

This is one of those things that is going to take a generation to change. It's a bit like changing to healthy kai. Bread is easy and goes a long way. Even though we know it is a bit bad for us, we can't just take it away and switch to salad overnight.

We need to talk about these things more and discuss them, so everyone knows what is expected. At the moment — even when I go to a home to uplift a body — it is automatic for people to kiss or harirū. Or it will be, 'Kia ora, Francis,' with a kiss from the wahine and a hongi for the tāne.

'Am I not good enough for a hongi?' a woman asked me once, when this happened. But it is just what we have got used to. So much so that it feels a bit weird giving a hongi to a woman. It shouldn't be.

I'm not saying this is something we need to do every day, like when we go into work and say hello to our colleagues. It should still be a bit special — for people we haven't seen in a long time, important visitors, after a formal ceremony or when whānau come into the funeral home, if I haven't met them yet.

It's about making people feel comfortable. If people want a kiss instead, they get one. But in the chapel here, I explain the hongi a bit and educate them. There is a fine line between being a funeral director and a tikanga Māori adviser. It's all in the same realm and how you convey the message is important. It's in the delivery, which needs to be subtle and gentle.

KAIORA
In my younger days in Te Tai Tokerau, we only saw males do the hongi. I was educated to think that was correct. Only later did I start to see many women do it, and now it is an everyday thing for wāhine. I like that. If you haven't seen someone for a long time and run into them at the bank or the doctor's or a café, you give them a hongi.

There are some people who are very staunch with their greeting. The hongi is their way of acknowledging and accepting someone when they meet them.

When it comes to people giving each other kisses, sometimes I feel awkward. You see them going in for the kiss and getting it wrong. There have been times when Francis has ended up kissing

In my younger days in Te Tai Tokerau, we only saw males do the hongi. I was educated to think that was correct. Only later did I start to see many women do it, and now it is an everyday thing for wāhine.

someone on the nose because he wasn't sure what was coming. 'I kissed Whaea on the nose! It turned out she wanted a hongi but I didn't know that, so I kissed her nose.'

There have been a couple of conferences where Francis and I have educated people on how to hongi. We have lots of examples from our own experience of what not to do — no kissing the eye, no kissing the nose, no rubbing your nose on the cheek.

It will be a long time before we see two Pākehā hongi each other as a normal greeting, but everything can change and people have already got used to many different things. Perhaps that will be one.

THIRTEEN

TAONGA

Taonga can have different meanings for different people. But it is always something you treasure. It can be your children or it can be a place. A taonga can be passed on and shared.

KAIORA

Taonga — what they mean and how they should be treated — need to be understood much better. Taonga means any treasure, but especially it is used to describe a gift of jewellery or something precious that is given to someone on a special occasion. They can be tangible or intangible, but they are always dear and sacred to you. A taonga can be given away but you can't sell it — you have to koha it. If a person wants to pass on a taonga, they must give it away to show the same respect with which it was given to them.

Our family's piece of whenua up north was given to my dad, not sold to him. My nan gifted him and his siblings a little homestead in Awanui. My aunty was living there and wanted to build on the land. She couldn't buy his share from him — he had to gift it to her.

When she passed away, it was given to her son. Then things went wrong. We noticed our whenua was about to get taken over by a bank because there was a mortgage on it and the payments had not been kept up. My sister put her hand up to buy it back. It was sad to see something that had been gifted having to be bought back.

Then our father gifted some land at Pawarenga to his children. He and my mum had brought up the first seven or eight of their children there. My mum was okay about being passed by when he gifted it to us. She knew she would move on to the life to come and it was for the next generation. We were to make use of it and treat it with respect. This was where he had taken a lot of our placentas and buried them. My father had laid down a rule that no drugs would be introduced on this land. No rubbish could be left down there. There was no road, so you had to use a quad bike or horse to get over the hill to our whenua.

We lived off the land. Dad provided for us by hunting or fishing. He always made sure his fishing rod was up to date. It was kept in a special place and none of us were allowed to play with it. It was his taonga, because he used it to provide for his whānau. If you went fishing, you had a karakia. If you went hunting, you had a karakia. Even now, the boys have a karakia before they go pig hunting. They usually come back with something.

There were about twenty-four horses on this land. If you wanted to go anywhere, you went by horse — and you first had to catch your horse. If the boys didn't have a horse, they had to carry the pig up the hill. You should have seen them struggling with that thing.

This same valley is also access for local people to go to Mitimiti. It is the way to the beach and popular with people going horse riding on their holidays.

People think something is public access because it is accessible. But if you are driving somewhere and see a gate along the way, you should ask yourself: Why is that gate there? Should I ask someone if I can go through there? There generally are signs around to say whether it is private property.

When my dad lived there, he would put a barrier up to stop people and often say to them, 'Who said you can come down here? This is my whenua. You need to go back up there, go around, go this other way. This is my land. My backyard. Do you see me ever crossing the back of your yard to take something over there? Have I used your pig dog this week? Don't take my horse. Same thing.'

He thought if he couldn't go on their land, they shouldn't be able to go on his. He didn't help himself to anything — even when he wanted to use the car door from an old wreck he saw, to fix his car, he asked permission.

He realised he needed a car to go to Kaitāia. He went to a cousin's house and said, 'I will swap you ten cows for a car.' It was hard for him to give away ten cows. But the cousin needed to think about it. Did he want cows? That is when we realised we were stepping up in the world, from walking or riding a horse to four wheels. He got the car, but twelve of us had to squash into it until we finally got a van in 1992.

Now there are twelve siblings who share this taonga that is our family land. Because there are so many people involved, we meet every three months to discuss what is being done with it and to put rules in place.

Taonga means any treasure, but especially it is used to describe a gift of jewellery or something precious that is given to someone on a special occasion. They can be tangible or intangible, but they are always dear and sacred to you.

For instance, if any of us build on the land, we have to think about the section and how close it is to where the others might be. All the siblings have a goal to build there. My brother tried to build twice and it got burnt down twice. This was a setback that was all to do with people who had been selling drugs in the area.

When my sister was ready to build, she came back to the trust — her siblings — and asked for permission. All of a sudden there were a few questions from the other sisters. Where would the whare go exactly? How much space was she going to use? I thought they were being a bit technical when we all owned the land together anyway. My sister was thinking about the next generation and all the others who would want access to this taonga.

* * *

If I was selling something — land or anything else — I would never describe it as a taonga. But some people use it in descriptions of their products. There is clothing now that has our language printed on it. I think this is beautiful. People are using our culture the best way possible for them and it is getting recognised.

I am in a business that sells things. Caskets are a taonga because they are your final bedding. I have seen caskets made out of woven flax but I have never seen those ones being purchased. They are always gifted.

Te reo Māori is a taonga and an example of the problem with putting a price on things.

At Te Wānanga o Aotearoa, you can study the language for free, which is beautiful, but at some institutions, you have to pay.

I understand you have to pay for your education, but some people just want to learn to te reo Māori.

Maybe because he got so sick, my dad had all the time in the world. He couldn't do much but he could donate his time and teach people what he could. His time was running out so he was giving it away.

It was a bit exhausting for Mum, having to look after him if he did wānanga all day. But he loved hanging out at the marae, sharing the taonga of his reo.

It can be good to make a point of calling things taonga — it means you treat them properly. My home, for instance, is a taonga. When people come to my whare, I like to make sure it is clean. People judge you if they come in your house and it is all dirty. But at same time, I like to have it so I can enjoy my space. I don't like to see things left around. If the kids leave their toys lying around, they need to learn not to. Those are their taonga. They know they should look after them.

There is a lot of tikanga around taonga. I worked at a big call centre for two years. They had many corporate clients, all being serviced in a massive space: Vodafone, Mercury, Contact Energy and Westpac were all there. There were inbound and outbound sales departments. I worked in inbound sales. They just came to you.

We had team meetings regularly. At one of these, a taonga was presented to a staff member to mark some achievement.

I wasn't too sure if they knew what they were receiving or giving. After the ceremony, if you could call it that, I asked the recipient if I could have a look at the taonga they had been given. It was a beautifully carved piece.

'Oh, that's beautiful,' I said. 'It's pounamu. Do you know where it is from? Does it come with something to tell you?'

'Oh, I should find out.'

'Yeah, that would be nice.'

I asked the team manager if he knew where it was from.

'Oh. Does it matter?' he said.

'Does it matter? Do you know what you've given her?'

'Yeah, it's a greenstone.'

'A greenstone from where?'

'Te Kauwhata? Is that where we got it from? Near Hamilton?'

'Usually, wherever you get greenstone from, there is a little description that comes with it.' It annoyed me that there was a taonga given, but not with full respect. There was no karakia. From there, I went to the supervisor of the floor, Henry.

'Sorry to disturb you, Henry, but I feel this is necessary.'

'Which team are you from? You've got to make an appointment.'

'I'm not making an appointment. I'm telling you what happened today is culturally inappropriate.'

I think Henry might have sighed.

'Okay,' he said. 'Take a seat.'

I felt there was a lot of ignorance behind all this but I could also see the intentions were good. I didn't want the person who got the taonga to feel uncomfortable. We talked through what it all meant and how it should be handled if someone was given a taonga in future. From then on, I became like a cultural adviser at the company.

'We are having a pōwhiri, Kaiora — can we have a karanga?'

'Okay. Can I have half an hour to educate everyone what it is?

'Half an hour?'

'Do you actually know what a pōwhiri is?'

'Yeah, a karanga and a song.'

'It's a bit more than that, bro, and I'm going to ask my husband to come in, and he will require a koha. If you are going to do this, I would ask that everyone be educated on what a pōwhiri is and what everyone's role is. Who is the tangata whenua? There are manuhiri — who is coming on with them?' Those things are important. I feel I woke them up a bit in that area.

A few years later, I bumped into the HR person who was there at the time and who had hired me.

'Didn't you rock that place a bit?' she said.

'Well, I was only a sales agent. I didn't become a team leader. I wasn't there that long.'

'We all talk about you still. And what you are doing now on TV is definitely educating all of us.'

I was always taught that it was important to know the whakapapa of a taonga. Did it have an ancestral link? If not, it needed to be blessed before it was worn. So when it was given without any ceremony or blessing, that felt wrong. In that case, it may have already been blessed but nobody knew. If any taonga is given to me, I will be told it is from Matua So-and-so who blessed it and wants me to wear it.

When Francis and I went to the Māori Business Leaders Awards and received the Māori Entrepreneurial Leader Award, they gave us beautiful pounamu from Ngāi Tahu that came with a description of the pattern and where the greenstone was from. I have worn it only once because I am scared to lose it. I feel it should be put up in a frame.

Receiving a taonga is easy. The responsibility it brings is another story. If I am wearing a taonga, I can't do anything that might look as though I am disrespecting it.

FRANCIS

Taonga can have different meanings for different people. But it is always something you treasure. It can be your children or it can be a place. It can be big or small. A taonga can be an item that is passed on and shared within a whānau. The whenua is also a taonga. It is a taonga to everyone.

My socks are very much a taonga to me, because it is so hard to find two that are the same when everyone in the house thinks they can share my socks.

We say a dead person is a taonga, too. To some people that is offensive and to others it is a beautiful thing to say. Te taonga o te mate is not a little thing we hand around, it is the loved one. It means you have been precious to me in my heart. Understanding the context is important.

There is a song called 'Taonga o Tōku Ngākau', which is taught in kōhanga reo. It's about treasuring your mokopuna even when they're being naughty because they're the dearest thing to your heart.

I am so grateful that through the years I have been gifted many korowai and greenstone taonga, but I'm not the sort of person to wear them, and I'm not sure why.

Receiving a taonga is easy. The responsibility it brings is another story. Especially in our day and age, when everything is videoed. If I am going to be at a staff do, there will be cameras around and I want to be able to have a good time and let my hair down. If I am wearing a taonga, I can't do anything that might look as though I am disrespecting it. So that is very limiting.

You have to live up to your taonga. I am not going to wear my beautiful greenstone and yell at someone down the road who overtook me without signalling. There is also responsibility when you give a taonga to someone else — they might not accept it if they think you were that person doing all the yelling.

KAIORA

So taonga can range from very important to quite trivial things, like the kids' toys. When we sing about taonga, that includes whenua, our waka, our maunga. We are kaitiaki of our taonga. We can't hold onto these things; they don't come with us when we move on. We leave them for the next generation. So we need to teach our children that these things are precious. The pounamu doesn't die. The moana doesn't die. We have to try to leave everything in a good state.

A work colleague once said to me, 'I've noticed, as Māori as you are, I don't see you wear a taonga.' I thought that was a big question for her to ask me.

'Do I need to wear it to be Māori?'

'Good question,' she said, and laughed.

'Yes, so was yours. If I come in tomorrow and I'm wearing a taonga, will I be more Māori?'

'Okay, it's getting a bit much now …'

I do wear taonga at certain events. I love pounamu but I have never bought any. Everything I have has been gifted to me. The only thing I have bought was mako shark teeth for kapa haka, when it was part of the uniform and not easy to find. Back then, I had to go to Te Kauwhata to get them. I don't wear them every day. And I don't have to wear them, or anything else, to be Māori.

FOURTEEN

MOKO

It's a really big deal getting it done — it is there for life and you are wearing the markings of your history.

KAIORA

Someone once said to me, 'Everyone in New Zealand except you and Francis has a tattoo.' The moko has definitely become more prevalent in the past ten years. You almost don't notice them on people now. Not quite, but we are getting there.

When I was growing up, moko were hardly seen. My dad had a first cousin, Uncle Mangu Rivers, who had some on his legs — puhoro. I thought it was very different, because I had never been exposed to tā moko.

Our father, being religious, never agreed for us to wear tā moko. He told us he appreciated that we didn't wear any, but that in the future we would encounter these same decisions and he left that to us.

In the Mormon religion, the body is a temple and you treat it as such — with purity and kindness. You can't use alcohol to clean it.

As children, when we came across people with markings on their face, it looked scary. But then I saw my parents embrace these people. They were whānau, so you couldn't be scared. My father would be angry if we showed fear: 'This is your uncle. Get over there and give him a hug.' Of course, he knew why we were scared, though no one ever said anything.

As a child, you don't get taught what moko are or what they mean until you go to a marae. You feel it is rude to ask.

There are some people that now stand out in my life who wear moko — tā moko or moko kauae. It expresses who they are and shows other people they are not afraid of that. It risks a lot of judgement and can come with a lot of stigma. But along with the negative connotations some people put on it, there usually comes a lot of mana and people respecting you.

Now it is becoming very normal. I have a lot of friends in the media who wear these and wear them proudly.

One is Francis's second cousin — Rukuwai Tipene-Allen. She was one of the first reporters with moko kauae on Māori Television.

She is ex-Hoani Waititi Marae. She grew up totally immersed in te reo Māori and now presents the news on TVNZ 1. When she presented lunchtime news for the first time, it was huge. Because of her role, she is an influencer. People are moved by what she and others have done. Maybe we will get to a point where if you are not wearing moko kauae or tā moko, you will feel left out.

Look at our Minister of Foreign Affairs, Nanaia Mahuta, and her beautiful moko kauae. Wow! She is getting a bit of flak for it, but it is maybe one in every 100 people. The fact that she is wearing moko kauae will be educational for the world. I love that she is taking it to another level.

I tell people I wear mine on the inside. If my mother got one, I would consider it. She is a role model. She is the matriarch and

I tell people I wear my moko on the inside. If my mother got one, I would consider it. She is a role model. She is the matriarch and she sets the standard for us.

she sets the standard for us. If I did it before her, I would feel I was taking that mana away. It is sacred. Maybe when she passes away, I might consider it. It is there as an option, but I feel right now that I'm good.

Some moko have their own whakapapa. Some have their own meaning. Or they can be personalised to your liking. Mostly, they are about your tūpuna and where you come from.

It's a really big deal getting it done — it is there for life and you are wearing the markings of your history. It can be a ceremonial process, with karakia and waiata. You will want to know your whakapapa well before you do it.

It is a false assumption to think someone who gets a moko kauae is radical. It is a statement, sure, but they are still the same person inside and almost out. It was probably more radical once. Now it is more mainstream.

There was a gathering recently for wāhine who wore moko kauae, where we live in Mt Albert. They were all there to embrace and uplift one another. It looked beautiful. I saw it on Facebook flooding my news feed and I did feel a bit left out. But these same wāhine respect who I am and would never pressure me.

FRANCIS

I said to my wife: 'Why don't I get my face done, and you get your moko kauae?' She looked at me like I was crazy.

'Come on — it would be great for our identity.'

'Nooo,' she said, and kept on applying her lipstick, foundation, eyeliner and all the rest.

I wasn't serious. I was just testing the water. We love it on others but we are not the type to wear it.

It used to be a shock to see a tā moko or moko kauae — there were some gang and prison associations with them. They were people who were prepared to cut themselves off from society and be seen as outsiders.

On social media, you see kōrero like: 'You shouldn't wear a moko kauae if you can't speak your tūpuna's language. You shouldn't wear it if you are going to drink or swear.' I am against that. They are like genes and eye colours — part of your family, whether you know te reo or not.

For the young people who are doing it, I sometimes wonder whether, because of the way we live, it is going to affect their life and job prospects. Will they be subject to systemic racism because of something so visible? There are lots of things about being Māori you can't see, but you can't not see that.

My wife and I blend with both worlds. Our skin is our identity. But where there is a moko, there definitely is a Māori. I hope those who have them use them wisely because they represent us all. From what I have seen, the people who wear them are very nice. They will help turn judgements around.

Education needs to take place to identify what the markings are. I don't have that knowledge. In our own whānau, a lot of people are getting moko kauae that mean something. We had that tradition, then lost it, and now it is back. One moment, we had no one and nothing — now there are all these indigenous representatives who are highly visible.

The next stage is whānau having wānanga to display what the meaning and origins of the moko are. People will be able to know by looking at them if they have had a bit of education.

We had that tradition, then lost it, and now it is back. One moment, we had no one and nothing — now there are all these indigenous representatives who are highly visible.

Soon, we will be having to deal with the question of Pākehā having moko. If I had a Pākehā wife and she wanted one, I would back her to death. The minute she and I consummated our marriage and became one, then my DNA has shifted into her and vice versa.

If I have children with this wife, they might decide to wear a moko. 'Why hasn't Mum got one? Because she's Pākehā?'

Having said that, I can't imagine a Pākehā woman who did not have a Māori husband just waking up and deciding to have a moko kauae. That would be shocking. Where is your connection?

In a way, that sort of thing is sad for Māori. First, we were angry because we couldn't be ourselves. Now we're getting angry because we have other people wanting to be us.

FIFTEEN

UTU

Utu is an action, not just a form of revenge, but also a relationship between two people. Something has been taken that needs to be restored. The restoration is utu.

FRANCIS

People think utu is about a revenge or compensation; an eye for an eye. The popular movie *Utu* gave that depiction of it. Today, when we use it, we are usually talking about settling your account. That is utu. Although the 'account' might not just mean money, especially in my work.

Here's an example. Sometimes people die with their heads up or on an angle, which means you can't get them to lie flat. When that happens, you need to use a deeper casket than you normally would. The head will fit and the lid won't hit the face. Or the legs may be on an angle and you need a wider casket.

I once had a body in a deep, wide casket, and presented it on a marae. As I started to leave, the people began a kōrero. So I stopped and waited. Someone was saying, 'Auē! Nui rawa to moenga. Ko wai e whai atu i a koe i roto i to kāwhena — I am

Utu doesn't always have to be negative. It just has to be a repayment, when something has happened.

looking at you, Whaea, in your casket that is too big and wonder who is going to go in there with you. We are asking for someone to join you.'

He thought the big casket was disrespectful. And it did look weird. He said what he said because some people were upset. They weren't angry. They were shocked.

That was the utu for putting someone in too big a casket — calling for someone else to join them in death. I thought, 'Oh my gosh.' When you have a good speaker and they have the ability to persuade people, everyone is thinking, 'Will it be me?'

Although Māori are great storytellers, we are great fib-tellers, too. One of the things about humans is that we naturally believe what we are told and people who know that can take advantage of it, especially in business and politics.

If something isn't done right on the way to the cemetery or during a funeral and tikanga doesn't prevail, utu means people will live with that for the rest of their lives. If anything bad happens, they will say, 'See, I got cancer because I didn't do this.' You know it is not the truth, but people will hold onto it. And I had a good reason to put that person in a big casket.

It is ridiculous but this is the power of a kaumātua. When you say something, it becomes suddenly real or law. The word 'utu' was used in his kōrero. He didn't understand why the casket was so large. But this scaremongering created a powerful impression. Educated people would know what is true and what is not, but others wouldn't. It's not the best example, but it shook me up. Afterwards, I went to the immediate whānau to explain why we did it. Apart from breaking her legs, there was nothing we could do.

They said they would rather she was comfortable, even if it meant she had to be placed in a larger coffin.

KAIORA

My knowledge of utu is minimal but I do know that, like many Māori words, it can mean a lot of things. Utu is an action, not just a form of revenge but also a relationship between two people. Something has been taken that needs to be restored. The restoration is utu.

Nowadays, that can commonly take the form of money.

When leaving PAK'nSAVE, my mum would say, 'Kua utu te nama — Have you paid?'

And I would say, 'Āe, ko utu — I have paid.'

So, it is not always something negative, with bad feelings involved. You replace something, and now that it is back in place, we are equal again. It doesn't have to be replaced straight away. There can be a long period before it needs to be paid back.

Back in the tūpuna days, it was actioned a lot. We would fight for land, for territory, for wāhine or taonga. If something was stolen, there was utu there. Sometimes it might be paid with a beheading.

If someone in your family is hurt, that could be very different. Especially if you don't feel the court system was adequate in dealing with it. A case close to us was Francis's cousin, Luke, who was killed in a fight when he was seventeen.

Utu doesn't always have to be negative. It just has to be a repayment, when something has happened. There is an imbalance between two people or groups of people and it has to be restored.

Luke's mother, Aunty Terry, was always about moving forward. She had a special strength that made her want to stop her other children lingering on the negativity of what took place. Her utu took the form of making something better than what had happened. She wanted to ensure her girls had something to live for and remember their brother by. That was her form of utu. She didn't seek retribution. She wanted people to honour Luke by living good lives themselves.

The justice system couldn't replace her son. There could never be enough compensation. So her ultimate utu was to ensure her children could be reminded of him and the good things he did.

A lot of the extended whānau wanted to see a different kind of utu. They wanted to see Luke's killer gone, to have same action done to him. But they also knew he had a history. He came from a whānau, too.

Utu doesn't always have to be negative. It just has to be a repayment, when something has happened. There is an imbalance between two people or groups of people and it has to be restored.

SIXTEEN

KOHA

You can koha kai, such as a beef, pork or sheep. You can koha your time in the kitchen. When you give, it will come back to you in other ways.

FRANCIS

Koha and utu sometimes go together. Utu can take the form of koha. When it is given from the heart, it is really beautiful. With Pacific Island funerals, people bring koha of food and money. These can be funerals costing $8000 to $10,000, and people pay their bill and put a koha on top.

In my heart, I think: How am I going to utu this? How can I restore the balance of this beautiful koha that has come in? I need to return this gesture, but I don't know how. I hope I will be able to some time in the future.

We give koha at birthdays, funerals and weddings. Mostly, these days, it is given in monetary form, but there are other things you can do to koha. You can koha kai, such as a beef, pork or sheep. You can koha your time in the kitchen. When you give, it will come back to you in other ways.

Thirty years ago, no family left their funerals bills unpaid, because the koha rolled in. Now, things are tough, and a lot of elders who provided guidance have died, so the koha system for tangihanga does not work as well. Unless the person who died is a rangatira, you can't rely on koha to pay for everything. People will turn up with koha but not in the amounts they used to. Back in the day, you could tally it up and find you had an excess.

Koha should always be an expression of aroha. It is not a set amount. Koha is beautiful but can be a nightmare if it is not used right. Some marae are koha-based — that is how they are funded. If you stay, you leave a koha. I wouldn't give only $50 for three nights, and you would hope that doesn't happen. But it does. So some marae are having to put down fees. Those who haven't respected the koha system have made this happen.

However, it is acknowledged by those receiving the koha that people will give what they can. 'E iti noa ana nā te aroha — It is small but given with love.'

I have been to tangi and done the koha collection. There are different ways to manage it. You can be that humble person and shake someone's hand and hand over the envelope in private. Some people do it when they do the hongi, because they don't want a big acknowledgement. Sometimes you have no choice. You have to do it on the marae after your speech — put it on the floor and stand back. People put down their koha and the tangata whenua will pick it up, say, 'Tēnā koutou,' and sit back down.

I have seen some people being overwhelmingly generous, and some giving coins as their koha. This stands out to me, because if they have to use coins, I know it has been tough for them to

Koha is usually seen as money, but mainly it is an action that comes from the heart, and it is given with love and respect.

gather their koha. That is probably their milk money or a cup of tea. They have made a sacrifice so they can give something.

When we stay at a friend's place — and Pākehā do this, too — we take koha in the form of something to eat or drink. Perhaps some staples like bread or milk, if we know they could be needed. But we wouldn't give our friends an envelope with money in it.

If you paint someone's house and say, 'Just give me a koha,' then you have to take what you get. I don't think it should work like that. If you have a proper job, you should have a proper fee.

In the rural areas, it is different. It astounds me how generous young people are to their old people. If they go diving, they will drop off pāua and kina to people like my nan. They mow her lawns or help with the weeding in the garden because that is getting hard for her to do. Nan knows to koha them, so she might dig up some food and make them a kai. But they haven't had to ask for anything.

It is important for givers to give without expecting anything in return. But if they are asked to do something, like paint a house, then they can and will expect something.

'Let's all come together and help Nan with her tomatoes, then when the fruits of the labour appear, we will partake.' That is the best sort of koha — leave the money out of it.

I was once involved with another kind of koha that I liked very much, when I was at school.

A lady from another country wanted a pōwhiri, and at Hato Petera this was the sort of thing we did all the time. Rent an iwi.

I think she may have been some sort of royalty from an Asian country. We were going to have the welcome in Aotea Square, with 120 of us there to give her a cultural experience.

She gave the school a donation, because that was how it worked.

Then she said she wanted to give every single pupil $500 on top of that. The school went crazy. We went crazy, and the school board went crazy, too. There was a big board meeting to discuss it because they didn't want to give the students the money. But her instructions were: here was this money for the school and she needed them to give $500 to each of the children. I think she said that if we didn't get it, the school wouldn't get its money either, so in the end they gave in and that was a very beautiful experience. I can't even remember what I did with the money, though I would have given some to Nan. The excitement of getting it was actually better than having it.

KAIORA

Koha is usually seen as money, but mainly it is an action that comes from the heart, and it is given with love and respect.

Koha doesn't always have to be in return for something. Giving it can be the first step in the process. My sister began doing weightlifting in Kaitāia a few years ago. She won some local competitions and qualified for the nationals. She messaged me: 'I am fundraising and I have got this raffle going at the moment. Would you be interested in buying a ticket?' She was raising funds for her weightlifting gear and flights and accommodation in Christchurch. Rather than buying a ticket, I said, 'I will give you a koha. You keep your tickets and sell them to other people.'

She was very emotional about it, but I wanted to koha her because she is someone who gives so much herself, not just in her whānau but around her community.

If you give koha and it's not in return for something, you don't assume you will get it back. It is a gift. I wouldn't ring my sister

As soon as you start talking exact amounts, it is not koha. My dad never liked us talking about figures. You put your money in the envelope and that's it.

up later and say, 'Any chance you can pay me back some of that money I gave you?' Then it would be utu.

And now we have things being called koha that once had other names, like school fees.

With the payments to marae, I was involved in a case where people had paid the koha, then a month later we got a letter asking when we were going to pay $350 for using the hall.

'What? I thought you said it was koha.'

'Oh yeah.'

'Didn't you get the money we gave on the day?'

'Yeah, but actually the hall is $500.'

I knew then that that person didn't understand koha, and I did feel a bit whakamā that they thought we hadn't given enough. I was the contact person for the booking because I made the initial engagement, but there was some misunderstanding with the use of the term.

As soon as you start talking exact amounts, it is not koha. My dad never liked us talking about figures. You put your money in the envelope and that's it. You don't say how much. But he would also always check how much was in it, and if he didn't think it was enough, he would try to put more in himself.

I was collecting for Francis's whānau at a tangi and things had got to the stage where I had to have a receipt book and keep a record of everyone's payments. They said they wanted it for their records so they could say thank you to people later.

At the end, there was a hui.

'Honey, can you read out the amounts people gave?' Francis asked me.

'No, you read it.'

'I don't like talking about money. I don't like using that word when it's about koha.'

So I had to read out what everyone had given. This whānau gave $100, this whānau gave $200, this whānau gave $10,000, this whānau gave $50, this whānau gave $20, this whānau gave $10.50.

When I read out the low amounts, I could hear people in the back cracking up.

'Did that whānau honestly give $10.50?' Francis asked, when I sat down again.

'Yes.'

The idea of reading everyone's koha out is that if someone's name isn't called, the whānau knows those people have not made a koha. So it is a check on that.

It used to be done differently and more formally during the whakatau, the official welcome speech, of the pōwhiri. You came on the marae, did your harirū and sat down. Someone spoke for your people and one of the males put the envelope on the ground in front of everyone, so everyone knew they had done it.

Everything is changing. People are using Givealittle for koha, and there is a link to send donations online. It is tidier and makes it easier to keep a record of what has been received, but it doesn't have the beauty of traditional approaches.

Although tangi might be the most common situation where this comes up, it can happen at any pōwhiri event. Weddings, for instance, or a whānau hui. You always take kai if nothing else. You don't go empty-handed. My dad's rule was that you should take enough to feed at least you and one other person. There is even a whakataukī about that: 'Ko tōu rourou ko taku rourou ka ora te iwi — If I give something and you give something, we are all happy.'

SEVENTEEN

TE REO MĀORI

Learning the language makes us complete — we can go back to the marae, hear conversations and understand them, reply to people. It feels beautiful.

KAIORA

Compared to how things were, even when I was growing up, te reo Māori is a lot more normalised today. It's more widely exposed. People are accepting it. Not so long ago, it was in serious decline.

I got more exposure to it when we started doing kapa haka and waiata at school. I loved doing waiata. They made learning fun. I was not just learning one plus one. You got to sing as you learnt. When it was getting near the time of the week when we did kapa haka, I would begin to get excited.

They only started this when I was in about standard one. School would ask my dad to come and advise. He tried to push for more te reo Māori in the schools but that didn't happen then. I had to go away to learn it. I didn't grow up totally immersed, even though he was a fluent speaker.

Dad didn't try very hard to teach me to speak te reo. Perhaps he thought it wasn't that essential, or he might have thought I would have picked it up later, if I went into a bilingual unit. My older sister was fluent and I think my father favoured her because of that. He put some effort into teaching her and I got jealous.

'Dad, I can do karanga, too.'

'Not now — your sister will be doing it today.'

But there was an occasion when she couldn't perform so he had to ask me to fill in. If that hadn't happened, he wouldn't have known I had any potential. I was determined to own it and I did. It was amazing. It felt so great to be on a marae and hear my name being spoken in the middle of a stream of te reo.

But I never got beyond being able to understand a certain amount of a kōrero and pick out a few words. I couldn't respond or have a long conversation with someone. Even at college, when te reo Māori had become more popular, I was envious of people younger than me who could speak much better. By then, the first kura kaupapa was operating up north, in Kaitāia. Seeing all those young kids running around speaking te reo Māori like it was their first language was so cool. I didn't like them knowing more than me, but it encouraged me to learn more.

After the death of my dad, who had been so staunch on teaching us about our culture, I lost touch with tikanga a bit. But it wasn't long before I began to feel something was missing in my life.

When I got to teachers' college, I wanted to learn te reo Māori and get back into tikanga. There was a course at Unitec called 'Te Reo me ngā Tikanga', which I signed up to. Once I was learning, I felt complete — I could go back to the marae, hear conversations and understand them, reply to people when they spoke to me, have a whole conversation. It felt beautiful. It was what my father had hoped I would learn, and at last I got it.

Now it is the turn of my children. I see a lot of myself in them because they aren't fluent either. They are just like me at the same age. They probably wouldn't be able to have a full conversation in te reo Māori, but they would be able to respond to commands and understand a lot.

It would be good for them to learn, because younger and younger people are being encouraged to get up and speak on marae now. There is a whole generation who are confident speakers with no nerves at all.

Things have come full circle. There has been a massive turnaround in how important it is. These days, Māori who don't have te reo are likely to be embarrassed. Even now, I get nervous when they ask to interview me on *Te Karere* and I know the whole thing will be in te reo Māori.

Sometimes at work, the phone rings and the person calling just starts in speaking te reo Māori fluently. Our receptionist isn't fluent and she has to ask me to get on the phone because she doesn't have a clue what they are saying.

But she wants to know what they are saying, so even she is going out of her way to learn te reo Māori and is loving her course.

I look at people like Stacey and Scotty Morrison speaking te reo Māori in their house with their whānau. We are trying in our own small way to encourage it at home — as a whānau, we learn a word every day and incorporate it when we can in our kōrero.

I don't like to force things on our kids. I would rather allow them to be part of it. Although, when we have karakia with whānau in the evening, the kids do have to be present.

I am grateful that our kids are exposed to te reo Māori at school. They learn waiata there and come home and sing them. If I don't know the particular waiata, I get a little envious. I want to be able to sing with them. That is one of the best things about waiata — singing together.

We certainly have more work to do with their te reo Māori in the home. They know plenty of commands, definitely — especially 'Sit down' and 'Shut up'. When I growl at them, they pretend they don't know what I'm saying, but I know they do.

In the early 2000s, there was a development that I didn't really understand. Te reo Māori was taught as part of a course called Te Panekiretanga and it was meant to be the next level. When you go to any marae, if you know te reo Māori you will be able to understand what most fluent speakers are saying. But then you get the ones who have graduated at Te Panekiretanga. It is amazing how many people don't understand these words.

I sit there thinking, 'Why can't you just say nui? Big is big. Why do you have to say ruarangi instead?'

You had to be nominated by your iwi to do this course. Some of the people who enrolled were already fluent in te reo Māori and teaching at uni but they wanted to know more and gain a different understanding. It's that group.

When I hear them, it is like they are talking to themselves. They are probably willing to give that knowledge outside their group, and I wish I'd had the opportunity to be part of it, but I am not interested in going out of my way to learn a new kind of reo when the one I know works okay for me and everyone I know.

Our kids know plenty of commands — especially 'Sit down' and 'Shut up'. When I growl at them, they pretend they don't know what I'm saying, but I know they do.

FRANCIS

I get flak for speaking a lot of English on the marae, but I want people to understand what I'm saying. I can speak till the cows come home in te reo Māori, but I feel like I'm talking to myself a lot of the time. 'Why is this guy always talking kōrero Pākehā?' my uncle once said. I will never be rude by speaking in a way people can't understand.

I have a message to get across. I want people to feel welcome. So I like to translate a lot of my kōrero.

When people understand te reo Māori, then we kōrero in te reo Māori. But there are many people — including most Māori people still — who don't understand, so why not translate my words into te reo Pākehā, do it in Māori and do it in English? There is no point talking if no one understands. I'm not there to talk to myself. So I will tell my pepeha and my whakapapa in te reo Māori, then translate it and give an explanation for why I have done it. If we can plant these seeds everywhere we go, we will see beautiful trees grow from them. We can't be exclusive. We have got to be inclusive.

Simple things can make a big difference to how people understand each other.

People ask me whether I think the language should be compulsory in schools. I think it should be available, but I don't think it should be forced on kids. I had it as an elective subject at school.

I think what should be forced on everyone is a marae visit. Every kura should go to a marae and learn a bit about the tikanga and kawa. I get blown away that so many New Zealanders haven't been on a marae. That sucks.

When New Zealanders go overseas, people say, 'Oh yes — All Blacks, haka.' That is all the tikanga they know about. Foreigners expect New Zealanders to know how to do a haka and turn one on for them. That's fine, but they should know what it means as well. And I want people to know what happens on a marae and be able to show that.

Schools go on camps every year. Some of those camps should be at marae, especially while we still have the old people there who have so much knowledge and are such good examples. Young people need to be given the opportunity to hear a karanga and get the goosebumps that you always get with that.

It shouldn't be too much. It shouldn't be shoved down their throats. The problem with compulsory *anything* is that if kids don't want to learn something then they won't learn it. You really can't make them. That's how it was for me with maths, anyway.

I do think encouraging younger ones to speak is very important and should be near the top of the list, so we will develop a nationwide understanding of te reo Māori. Funerals and tangi are where you see the culture at its strongest. People come out of nowhere to support one another and the culture is central to this.

And not just on marae. When I take a body to a house for a home funeral, if there is no Māori language being heard, it feels weird. More and more often people ask me to help — the mourners feel they need a prayer or hymn in te reo Māori.

We need to keep the tradition alive through the generations, not let it die out with the aunties and uncles who are around today.

We have so many Māori politicians in Parliament now; it will be interesting to see what they do about our language and culture.

Funerals and tangi are where you see the culture at its strongest. People come out of nowhere to support one another and the culture is central to this.

It's not hard to visit a marae and learn what wharenui means — not just the word, but what the building is for and the symbolism of all its parts. And when those people travel, they can share that knowledge about their country.

KAIORA

When it comes to te reo Māori, I see pronunciation as another word for respect. I don't expect people to get it right all the time, but I like them to try.

Schools have a big part to play in this. Some lack Māori teachers or any teachers with knowledge of Māori culture. There is a big need for these teachers at all mainstream schools.

There are a lot of teachers who do understand what is needed and work hard to make it happen. I have aroha for those teachers. They end up being seen as advisers across the whole school. If anything goes wrong at a pōwhiri or with anything kaupapa Māori, they get the growling when they have just been trying to do the right thing.

At our local primary school, they are doing their best. They ask Francis and me if we can fill in with a karanga here or a kōrero there, and we try to help.

I get a bit concerned if any of our boys are being taught something different from what they learn at home. Mikae came back with a word in Māori Language Week once. It didn't sound right.

'What was that again?'

He said it again. It was just the pronunciation that was the problem.

'That's not it, son.'

He was so adamant because it was what he had been told at school: 'That is how you pronounce it.'

'Maybe Mummy needs to talk to your teacher and tell her how it is supposed to be said, because everyone is going to say it wrong.'

'But you're wrong.'

I decided to leave it at that. Almost. I did email his teacher and say, 'I know you are doing your best, it's just that this is wrong and this is right,' and she did thank me.

Then there's my name. In the Air New Zealand Koru Lounge, when you order a coffee, you type in your name and they call it out when your drink is ready. More than once the barista has said, 'Here you are, Kia ora.'

'Some people need to learn to read,' I thought. I know I typed in my own name correctly.

'If you look properly,' I said, 'it is a before i. It is Kaiora. Kia ora is not my name.'

'Oh my gosh, I'm so sorry.'

'It's okay. I get that often.'

It is a bit of a bummer. I had it at school when teachers would call out Kia ora not Kaiora. But my mum came in one day and said to the teacher, 'Right, my daughter's name is Kaiora. You can say *Kai-ora*'— and she tried to teach her how to pronounce it. From then on, teachers tried to say it properly but it left a funny taste. Those around me thought it was funny to continue to call me Kia ora, when they knew how to pronounce my name correctly.

When I got to college, it was still the same. Some teachers pronounced it perfectly. Others, not so much. And my peers would continue to mock, calling me Kia ora. A teacher called me Kiore once, and my peers laughed even longer, because kiore means rat. It was upsetting for a while. Those close to me helped me through it. Then they gave me a special nickname — Iore — which was short for Kiore, but only they and I knew what it meant.

This is why I let a lot of people just call me Kai. It's better than having them butcher my name.

Legally, it's still not quite right, because on my birth certificate my mum wrote Kai-ora. But I was raised to write it as one word and I really can't be bothered getting it changed. Especially if there are people who won't pronounce it properly no matter what I do.

People often ask me to correct their pronunciation. I have been corrected myself plenty of times. I'm used to giving the proper pronunciation now because I was growled at so often. I was told I was disrespecting other people and the tikanga.

I learnt a good lesson about this when I was working in Peeni Henare's Parliamentary Services office, before I had gone to work with Francis. Francis texted me and asked me to order some caskets for him. I had the time, so I rang Western Caskets.

'Could I please have six reemoo caskets and six cowree ones?' I gave the order and hung up.

'Did you just say reemoo?' asked my workmate.

'Yeah. Because that's how Western Caskets are used to hearing it.'

'But it's rimu. If you're going to order something, you're going to say the name. And it's not cowree, its kauri. If you ring from this office and are going to say Māori words, you're going to say them correctly.'

She was right. I did feel a bit ashamed. I knew how to pronounce the words properly.

I see pronunciation as another word for respect. I don't expect people to get it right all the time, but I like them to try. If their intentions are good and they have a good heart, I don't feel so bad.

I rang the casket people and said, 'I'm not making this a big deal but from now on I'll be pronouncing words correctly.'

'That's good to know. A lot of us here would appreciate it because we can start pronouncing the words correctly, too. You will encourage us. Thank you, Kai.'

It's very embarrassing getting told off by your own. When it comes to non-Māori people and their pronunciation, how I feel if they get it wrong depends on how they are expressing it. If their intentions are good and they have a good heart, I don't feel so bad.

I know they don't mean to disrespect the word. It's probably because they don't know how to say it. But if they want to be educated on how to say something properly, I am definitely there to help.

I know a funeral director down the line. He practically has a monopoly in his area. He has a bit of Māori in him and his girlfriend is Māori. He doesn't like it when people think he is just Pākehā. I said, 'Maybe if I helped you pronounce words properly, you'd get more people. Maybe that's why the Māori market don't come to you.'

Maybe it would help everyone if we did have compulsory te reo. I disagree with Francis on this. I really like that idea. It would benefit not just our kids, but as all those kids get older, te reo Māori will be stronger in the whole country. Anyone who doesn't know the basics will feel left out.

EIGHTEEN

KAI

If someone brings you food, you will always eat some, so as not to offend, because they have gone out of their way to put it on, and are being kind.

FRANCIS

I love kai, as most people know, and I love Māoritanga. Kai is a very important part of many events, especially tangi. But there is a lot of Māori kai I just can't get my head around and this can create problems. Also, Kaiora and I have very different tastes, although that doesn't create so many problems because if we are somewhere and there is something I can't eat, she will usually finish mine as well.

I like kūtai, mussels and pāua, but they have to be cooked. I will eat crayfish, but just the nice clean parts, like the tail. Kaiora eats the guts and everything else.

I wish I could eat kina, because I see how much people like my wife and our whānau enjoy it. It is a beautiful sight. Even Mihaka, who is a fussy eater, says, 'Mum, can I have some?' when he sees her, because she makes it look so yummy, like yoghurt. But I prefer her to eat them fresh. If they are a couple of days old, she starts farting and it's awful. You can ask my staff.

I ate plenty of fish growing up, because we lived near the sea. I loved flounder and kahawai. Pop would get a lot of those at the beach. Nan would fry the flounder in butter and we would have it with takakau bread. It was a standard part of what we ate. It's a nostalgic type of kai when I eat it today. The good memories come flooding back.

Takakau is one of my favourite foods. How traditional it is, I'm not sure, but it has been a staple on the marae for a couple of generations in my experience. It didn't have a lot of nutritional value, but it sure filled the gap and helped make the other food go further. Nan makes it with just flour and water, cooked in an oven or in the ground or deep-fried.

I gave some that my nan had made to my Sāmoan friends at work.

'Have this — it's so yummy,' I said.

'Francis, it tastes like nothing.'

They were right. I forgot. It was like the first time I had taro. For me, takakau is nostalgic — it is about more than just eating bread.

Nowadays, I see lots of rēwena in bakeries — another Māori tradition that is becoming part of wider culture.

At Pawarenga, Pop had a cow and milked it. We had milk on tap. Every morning before school, for breakfast I had a sop — warm milk with two or three slices of bread and sugar that you stir around till it gets all sloppy. I loved that in the morning, especially when it got cold. Now I think: What the hell was I doing eating that? It was so bad and unhealthy with the amount of sugar I had.

But it was a cheap breakfast because there was always lots of milk for it.

Christmas dinner was always amazing, although it wasn't very traditional. If Nan had any pāua, there would be pāua and cream. There was always beetroot that Nan grew herself. Every time I see beetroot it reminds me of Christmas. I know beetroot isn't very flash, but anything is special if you only have it at Christmas. When McDonald's have the Kiwiburger — which has beetroot in it and is not available all year round — I always have that.

Because we don't go up there as often as we used to, when I do go to Nan's she spoils me. The other week I was up there to drop a mate off, and at 10 a.m., she had a roast pork ready with beetroot. And her home-made pickle, which I don't really eat. The beetroot was out of a tin but it was her way of putting on a little feast.

There is only her in the house, and she is lonely, so when someone comes she goes all out. In my own home now, a special-occasion dinner with the whānau will be roast pork. Always two of them. And a pavlova as well. It is the abundance that makes it special. The time that has been taken, starting to prepare the kai in the morning, the time the whānau will spend together enjoying it.

I often think about how our people die and at what age and the sicknesses they have. Then you go back to the marae and see what we people used to eat there — lots of bread, fried bread, bread stuffing, bread pudding. Hāngi wasn't so bad. Boil-up was not so bad, but then you had the doughboys with it. They helped stretch the budget, but they didn't help stretch the lifespan.

Maybe in the very old times marae food was healthier. White sugar and flour didn't get here till the Pākehā brought them.

Nan would fry the flounder in butter and we would have it with takakau bread. It was a standard part of what we ate.
It's a nostalgic type of kai when I eat it today. The good memories come flooding back.

Now we need to change our diet again and I think it will need to be generational.

Once, I was embalming a gentleman who died at home. He was only 58. He had diabetes and his leg was black from lack of circulation. I wondered why they hadn't cut it off. It must have been so painful. He must have suffered terribly. If they had cut if off, he might have had a better quality of life. I could smell his toes from the car. These are the kinds of issues we are dealing with thanks to soft drinks and junk food.

Kids get so much pressure to eat and drink bad things that make them sick in later life. But not everything that is healthy is expensive. At the supermarket, they sell five-litre cartons of water that come with a little dispenser. It is a lot cheaper than little bottles of water. You put it on your bench and everyone helps themselves. When it's empty, you get another one. I know plastic's bad but you just can't get everything right all the time.

If that's what kids get used to, when they do get a fizzy drink, they appreciate it.

We are doing that as a tikanga at home — drinking water plus physical activity. We started doing this so we could feel we were doing a better job as parents. We've also cut back on phone time.

The TV show has made some things about food even more complicated. Because I am a bit of a celebrity, when I go to a hui mate, I always get put near the top and offered all the choicest kai. But that means all the best kina, pāua and other things I don't like. They get piled up in front of me and then everyone sits back and waits for me to eat it.

There is a lot I wouldn't eat if I had the choice, but if someone brings me anything at all, I will eat some so as not to offend, because they have gone out of their way to put it on, and I know they are being kind.

I was once brought twelve oysters.

'Francis, these are for you from Aunty over there.' And there was Aunty, smiling and giving me a little wave.

'Oh, thank you, Aunty. I am so full. Let me just have one.'

And I did. To me, oysters are just like a bit of water, salt and snot.

'Oh, that's great, Aunty — they are so fat.'

This is the bit Kaiora loves — when she gets to finish all the seafood that has been set aside for me. All the kina and pāua are piled up in front of me. How offensive to sit there and not eat it. So I have my wife there and slip it to her. I say, 'Oh, the kina is so fat. I can't eat them — that is the hard part.'

This is often on the last day of the tangi or the celebration and you know people have gone diving especially for these things. People actually make time to fill the boat up, get the gear and go diving. At that point, the whakamā overcomes me — the shame of not being able to partake. This is what happens if I am attending a hāngi just as myself.

But even when I am only there as the funeral director, the hosts think they have to feed me. Everyone has to have a kai at the hākari. I will always be offered something and it is considered rude if I don't take it. And sometimes I am just full and don't want to eat anything.

If I'm not going to sit down and have a kai, they will pack it up for me to take away. I walked out with five containers once. I tried to explain I was the only one there. 'No, Francis. Take it with you and give to the others.'

Francis struggles — every time I eat fish heads, with the sloshy sound it makes, it's like he is going to vomit.

I felt terrible walking back to the car with everyone looking. I was sure other people needed the kai more than I did.

On the marae, there are so many food issues to deal with. It's not just what you eat, it's how much. It's what people use to show respect and affection. The bigger the pile of food, the more love they are expressing. That's how people see it.

But we also need to give people permission not to go overboard. Why are we really here: for the carbs or to remember our friends? Some people say they're just going for the free hāngi. We have to change that.

'It's our tikanga,' say the old people, as they pile up their plates. Bull. The tikanga is to make sure you have some food to go through your body to uplift the noa. A cup of tea and a sandwich is enough. I am seeing more urban marae doing that. It's partly for health and it is partly for financial reasons.

At Pop's headstone unveiling, we had grazing tables and you helped yourself. This is new. Traditionally, the kai was served up and everyone got a big portion. Now you can just take what you want. This is an example of how Pākehā and Māori can each learn from the other's culture. Yes, Māori are wonderful at mourning and grieving, but we have problems in the kitchen with the food. Pākehā could do with some help mourning, but I love the way they do the food and reception.

Another issue with kai that we often lose sight of is how much it costs. It is hard for many families to eat properly with the budgets they are on. Unhealthy food is cheap and good food is expensive. Temptation is everywhere you look. There is a fast-food place or someone selling sugary drinks at every corner.

KAIORA

I love all kaimoana, much to my husband's distress. One of my sisters and her husband go fishing a lot, and we benefit from that. Well, I benefit from that. Francis struggles — every time I eat fish heads, with the sloshy sound it makes, it's like he is going to vomit. When I boil them up in the pot, the smell permeates the whole house, but I absolutely love them and eat every bit. My favourite part is the eyes. He knows if he wants to make me happy, all he has to do is get a couple of fish heads. The funny thing is that about the only seafood I don't like is scallops and Francis eats them.

How lucky we are to be able to choose to eat food we like. When I look back to my own childhood, I can see my dad didn't have much choice about food for us. He needed to fish a lot and to go pig hunting to provide for us.

When he got sick and couldn't do it himself, he sent my older brothers out hunting and fishing when we needed kai. There was always a lot of shellfish: kina, kūtai, pipi. If we went to the beach, we all had to get some pipi before we were allowed to have a swim, or get kūtai before we were allowed to play. We all had to get at least a hatful or fill up our shirt and walk it back to the house. It was probably about two kilometres away. That was quite a distance at that age with your pockets full of seafood. If you had a bag to put everything in, you were rich as.

Everyone had to do their bit, and it felt like we did it every week. It was good because it meant if we were really hungry for kai, we knew how to get our own.

My mother made brawn and I didn't even know what it was until I saw her cooking it when I was a teenager. It was just another thing we had been eating for years. If we had a sports event, we were given brawn and told it would make us stronger and faster. We would smash it back before school and be sure we would win our race because of it.

It's amazing how well our parents did finding food out of nothing to feed us all. We hardly ever saw store-bought loaves of bread. Mum always made it. We hardly ever saw milk bottles or cartons because we always had milk powder.

I love muttonbird now, though I didn't see much of that growing up. I saw a lot of pigeon. Watercress was always handy. In our garden, there was lettuce, tomato, potato, kūmara, corn, cabbage, watermelon. We felt rich.

And we all had our little areas to look after. Next door to us was an empty patch of land, and our dad used to grow food on it. No one complained.

When Mr Whippy came, we gave him a bag of kūmara in exchange for ice creams. He didn't come every week because he would have ended up with too much kūmara.

In my bit of garden, there were kūmara and watermelon growing next to each other. If I didn't have an apple to take to school, I would help myself to a watermelon.

One of my friends didn't believe I had grown it myself, so I brought her home and got my dad to tell her.

'Give her a watermelon if she wants,' said Dad, and I did.

Then my friend's dad came back with her and the watermelon: 'My girl said you gave her this — I just want to make sure she hadn't stolen it from you.' She was crying, like her dad really thought she had stolen it.

Muttonbird was a delicacy in our house because they weren't easy to come by. Once a year, when they were in season, our dad would go and knock on someone's door — I don't know how he sourced them to be honest, but he found them.

I remember it being so salty. You are supposed to boil it twice but he only boiled it once. He boiled everything — even beautiful pieces of pork.

But there was one thing I wouldn't eat — rotten corn. I still can't, to this day. If there was rotten corn being prepared, we could smell it down the street before we got home. We never went into the house on those days. We stayed outside playing. Eventually we had to go in, but the smell was still so bad it stopped us sleeping.

Francis does not like any of these things, full stop. He won't even eat fresh fish if he can avoid it — he prefers Filet-O-Fish from McDonald's.

They filmed me eating some fish heads and kina for *The Casketeers*. I had Fehi, one of my colleagues, next to me. She was amazed.

'How do you eat that stuff?'

'Do you mind? This is a delicacy and I hardly ever get to eat it.'

We had boiled the fish heads, and from downstairs that was all you could smell. I knew Francis would come back and say he was very disappointed that there was this smell in the funeral home. I demolished them and did lots of spraying around so the odour was gone by the time he got back.

My kids are like their dad — totally not into traditional foods, with the exception of Mihaka, who loves seafood. The others might favour the pāua and cream but that is about it. Baby Francis hasn't taken a liking to any of them.

* * *

A hākari is important to finish any process. It feels wrong if there is no kai at the end, even if you have just been sitting down and having a kōrero with someone. It is an important part of manaaki.

A hākari is important to finish any process. It feels wrong if there is no kai at the end, even if you have just been sitting down and having a kōrero with someone. It is an important part of manaaki. If there were visitors and there was not much food, Mum would always whip up some fried bread and that would go a long way.

Kai is important at the end of tangihanga, not just because of lifting the tapu and returning to noa, but also because during the ceremony you haven't been able to talk to people who you might not have seen in a long time. You see them arrive and all you can do is give them a wave because the ceremony is taking place. Now you are getting together and catching up, and kai helps you do that.

It's also a chance to heal. Maybe the mate has brought people together so that they can sort things out and fix any mamae that there is between them.

You are judged on your kai, I know. Another thing my dad taught me was that if you have invited ten people, you should cater for twenty. Make sure you have more than enough for everyone. If you have leftovers, then you have some kai for the next day.

NINETEEN

HEROES

It makes us proud to be Māori listening to our music and the stories told through song and dance and haka. It is another way in which we are able to express tikanga.

FRANCIS

Kids need heroes. And Māori kids especially need Māori heroes because they see a lot of negative stereotypes of our people and need to be reminded that there are Māori heroes, too.

When I was growing up with no TV and no movies, my heroes were really the people I was exposed to. And because I was living with my grandparents, I was exposed to a lot of elderly people. Later, when I moved to Auckland, I got different heroes, especially people who were prominent in the worlds of music and te reo Māori.

My grandparents are my biggest heroes because they taught me all I really need to know in life. They showed me how to live within your means and be thankful for what you have. Thankfully, I am grateful for power and a toilet and running water, but having been brought up with very little I know we can live without it.

But mostly my pop was a very kind and gentle man. I hope some of that has come through to me.

Nan was a firm lady. They say you marry someone like your mother and I think my wife and her are quite the same. They are true to their own tikanga, making sure things are done right, are firm and not shy to say no if they need to. Nan was the pillar of faith in the family. With my own children, my wife is the faithful one who keeps us all in line and makes us remember about the power higher than us.

Growing up, we only listened to the races on the radio so I didn't have sports heroes or music idols. In the early days. I wasn't one of those tamariki running around pretending to be an All Black.

I love people who are orators, especially ones who can converse in both languages and express them both beautifully. The broadcaster Julian Wilcox is an incredibly talented orator. When you are speaking te reo Māori, you have to think everything back to front and around and around and upside down. To be able to turn that around in your brain and translate it so it is understandable in beautiful language — not just word for word — is a huge challenge. He's got that. I will always watch and listen to anything with him in it. I've had the privilege of being interviewed by him a couple of times.

I also love Peeni Henare, another eloquent translator whose te reo Māori is so poetic and so beautiful. Some of the things that come out of his mouth make you feel like you are listening to the tūpuna of old. His mind is very creative and his speech is very uplifting. It is about raising other people up — never himself. You wouldn't expect that from a politician, but when he speaks at events it is always about the subject at hand and glorifying it.

I have seen a lot of Māori people sitting there listening to him, just blown away. He is like a modern-day Māori Shakespeare.

Once I started doing kapa haka I became a huge fan of many kapa haka groups: Te Waka Huia, Te Whānau-ā-Apanui, all the big powerhouse groups. Again, I admired all their skills, whether they were doing very simple tunes or the most difficult ones. A lot of groups would get popular songs and use the tune to create Māori songs — men singing their parts, the women theirs, like a choir where everyone has to grab a note and run with it.

It made me proud to be a Māori listening to our music and the stories they told through song and dance and haka. It was another way in which we were able to express tikanga — through story and dance. We keep our culture alive doing kapa haka.

Peeni and Julian are part of the te reo Māori resurgence. They are among the first kura kaupapa students who have left and gone into Māori TV, news and current affairs. We need more of these people encouraging te reo Māori.

At work here, through prayer and song and hymn, we do our little bit to make sure families are comfortable with te reo. In the past, I had a rule that if a Pākehā family walked through the door we had to say, 'Hello and welcome.' If a Māori family walked in, we would say, 'Kia ora.' Everyone gets a kia ora now.

I have heroes for tikanga — Mana Epiha, the director of *The Casketeers* series four, is one. If I want guidance on any issue, I have a lot of people I can call on. Mana, Julian and Peeni could all fill that role, but usually I would text Peeni: 'Kia ora, bro, when you get a moment ...'

Before them, it was my Uncle Dodi. He is such a beautiful man. When I ask him for guidance, he always says, 'What do

Māori kids especially need Māori heroes because they see a lot of negative stereotypes of our people and need to be reminded that there are Māori heroes, too.

you think? If you feel like it's right, it's right.' But usually I prefer someone to say, 'This is the way you do it.'

I also have people I admire in the funeral business. If I need advice on typical Pākehā funeral etiquette, I can call on a knowledgeable person named Terry Longley, who does mainly European funerals. Brad Shaw is another. Their creativity with funerals and the way they are changing them is amazing.

KAIORA

My dad was my hero, of course. No one has been able to fill his shoes since he passed. There were aunties and uncles around, but they started dying too, and no one's guidance was ever quite the same as the lessons we got from Dad.

I admire my mum because she raised twelve of us on her own when Dad died, just after I had turned eleven. She didn't have a job at the time because when he got sick, she had to give up her work to care for him. There were no home dialysis machines then, and Kaitāia Hospital didn't have the facilities. So she had to travel to Whangārei every Monday, Wednesday and Friday for his treatment. Then, when he was gone, she had to go out and look for a job to feed us, after six years out of the workforce. We all helped. The eldest one had to chip in with her wages. I was twelve when I got my first paper run, and I gave $10 out of my $12 a week to Mum. I admire her for how she got on with things.

When Mum went back to work, it was in the health area as part of a new Māori health trust called Te Hauora o te Hiku o te Ika, which means tail of the fish, meaning that it is for the Far North. Aunty Muriwai was a mover in that. It now has several parts, including a health clinic and a social services arm.

These women had a vision — Mum, Aunty Muriwai and Aunty Tilly — and they made it happen. Sir Graham Latimer was involved. They got a member from each iwi — Ngāti Kuri, Te Rarawa, Ngāti Kahu and others — to form a board. They gave scholarships to people on the condition they would come back and work in the community for a while at the end of their studies. These women didn't just sit around. They may have come from small communities, but they had some big ideas and made them happen.

My Aunty Matire, who we called Tilly, was our dad's sister, and used to fight a lot with him about his Mormon faith. She was another one who would talk on the marae. This was the beginning of things changing. You could do that on your own marae but you couldn't do it on any other marae, unless you could connect to it in some way.

I have been blessed with good advice and counsel from the heroes in my family. My Aunty Christine, who passed away a year or so ago, is someone else I looked up to. She told me I had a job to do. She believed everyone has a purpose and I am yet to complete mine, which is to continue to serve our people, not just in the funeral industry but also as an adviser.

When we started Tipene Funerals, she was at the opening of our branches. She would always be our guidance for tikanga and te reo in the funeral homes. She and her husband, Pio, were stores of knowledge. We are not from Tāmaki Makaurau but they raised their tamariki here and had an understanding of the rohe. They had served their time and established relationships with tangata whenua and were able to give guidance to many communities here in Auckland.

She had a role with the Waitematā DHB as part of kaumātua kuia rōpū. She was a tutor in te reo Māori at Unitec.

If we were in trouble of any kind, she and Pio were the ones to get advice from. They could tell us about the right positioning of the tūpāpaku in the whare, or when it was right to give the mana to the whānau at the funeral home. Do we need to have a kōrero with the whānau first, or whakatau? Can we just let them stay the night?

A lot of older Māori look out for younger people, who they think can make a contribution to their people. She was so that person. She was all for the next generation.

The elderly are often set in their ways. That is fine. They want to preserve tradition. She was different, as she showed when she decided she wanted to be cremated.

I always respect people whose actions will make things better in the future. Aunty (and Dame) Naida Glavish is also one who I admire for being staunch and someone who has made things happen.

Jacinda Ardern is someone I admire enormously. I can't think of any other prime minister we have had who would have been able to face the amount of challenges that have come up in her time as leader. I like her values. I like that she says it is important to be kind, and that you can run the country and have a baby.

I have been to the Māori Business Leaders Awards three times and met some very inspiring women there. The first time, I couldn't believe we had been invited. We just ran a small company and here we were on a red carpet with people all dressed to the nines.

I was sitting next to Manuka Henare, who was a professor at the University of Auckland Business School. I got a big surprise when he was called up as guest speaker.

'I didn't know who he was,' I said to the woman sitting on my other side.

'Didn't you read the pamphlet?'

I didn't get a pamphlet.

I remember Mavis Mullins winning the Outstanding Māori Business Leader Award. She is part of founding 2degrees, runs a farm business and has a TV show as well. And she has a family on top of all that, like me. That's what captured me. I thought if she can do it, so can I. I had just had Nihaka and was feeling run down. Then I looked at this wonderful woman who had so much to give, and I felt I could do the same.

I wanted to get a photo with her but I didn't that night; I was a bit shy with all those people.

A couple of years later, Francis and I won an award. That evening we met Whaea Pania Tyson-Nathan, who was CEO of Māori Tourism. She is another wonderful wahine who has achieved a lot, but you could hear the humility in her voice. She said to me, 'I've heard so much about you. I'm sorry I've never watched your show, but my staff tell me how amazing you are and if I could get a photo with you that would be amazing.'

'Oh, but I want a photo with you — you just won the big award.'

A month or so after that, she sent us seven boxes of cookies and a note: 'I finally watched the show. Please enjoy the biscuits.' Francis didn't have to buy any biscuits for a long time, and no one was fighting over biscuits or stealing them.

Wāhine like this are the reason I love that Beyoncé says girls run the world. Go Beyoncé! She is another artist who has composed, had children, runs a business and is dominating

I thought if she can do it, so can I. I looked at this wonderful woman, who had so much to give, and I felt I could do the same.

around the world. She has so many messages to share that I can relate to. She has a song called 'Grown Woman', about how she can do whatever she wants. She had to take steps to get to that point and needed people to guide her, but now she knows and doesn't need to be told what to do any more. She is a true feminist.

And then there's Iron Man. I love Iron Man for his heart. There is that big machine to keep his heart going, and when that has gone, he is no one. I used to use the lesson of that heart when the big kids were younger. I would say, 'You've hurt my heart. Iron Man is dying now.' They would run around to try to find a heart because Iron Man was their favourite.

TWENTY

WHAIKŌRERO

Oratory keeps our culture alive. It keeps our language in its best form. We are able to recite whakapapa; we are able to share our identities, our stories, our love and our hate.

FRANCIS

I can see that the new generation will take on the task of reviving the great Māori tradition of oratory. When you go to Hoani Waititi Marae in Auckland, with its well-established kura kaupapa, you see such confident and fluent young people. To sit back and hear them speak is amazing. They are happy to talk in te reo Māori, even if they don't have much to say yet. But the kura are pockets. Most Māori children are not in kura kaupapa but in mainstream schools.

If you look at Māori Television or TVNZ, their broadcasters are kura kaupapa kids, and a lot are from Hoani Waititi. Both our executive producer and director on *The Casketeers* are kura kaupapa people.

The tradition of oratory in my own family was unique. I never heard my grandfather speak te reo Māori in public. I don't know why. His brothers spoke comfortably, but there seemed to be an understanding that he wouldn't. When we went onto a marae as a whānau, my uncle would look at me to speak, not at Pop.

'You talk.'

So my grandfather never spoke on the marae or in any other public setting. He and my nan were both very quiet people. Like other talents, skill at oratory can miss a generation or two. He has a grandson and other mokopuna who talk quite a bit. It all balances out in the end.

But I used to get annoyed at this. There were many times when my uncles stood and spoke, but never my grandfather. 'Why doesn't Pop ever stand up and say something?' As life went on, we got used to it and it wasn't annoying anymore. I became one of the people who would talk in Pop's place. We had given up on ever hearing him speak.

Then one Christmas, at my cousin Darcy's in Pamapuria, when it was just the immediate family getting together, when we had given up all hope of ever hearing him do it, he did speak. It wasn't a big ceremony on the marae or some important public occasion. It was just Christmas with the whānau. What a special gift that was.

He spoke in te reo Māori. He started with a mihi to everyone and I can't even remember much of what he said, but I do remember there were tears flowing down all our faces to hear Pop talking. I was just blown away.

We were in a little gazebo that had been put up for Christmas. We had a microphone and he used that. I'm just so happy we got to see it. It confirmed that he knew what to say and how to say it. I don't know why it happened. I'm just glad I saw it.

Oratory is important on the marae because it does a lot of different jobs. It is how you learn about what is right or wrong in a public setting. If you, as a tāne, get up and give your opinion, fine. And you will get a lot of opinions back. This is the right place for that.

You may be there to pay your respects at a funeral, and the whole kaupapa turns into a discussion of politics. You are allowed to do that. You express your thoughts and get the feedback.

Others will share their kōrero and tell you what their tūpuna did, and you can learn from those examples. It's better than listening to someone saying do this, do that, don't get a moko kauae if you aren't fluent in te reo Māori.

I don't know anyone who says they are a fluent orator. Some people think I sound fluent. It's not true. Just when you think you know it all, someone comes along and says something in te reo Māori that is so beautiful and so moving it blows you out of the water.

Sometimes, when you are having your kōrero or whaikōrero in a formal setting, it is like you are having your one chance to be in a Hollywood blockbuster. Get it right and you will have a brilliant career. Get it wrong and it's all over for you.

The pressure that one feels before doing a whaikōrero is huge. There are people who aren't bothered at all. It is just another kōrero for them. Those people are blessed. Our superstars are these kaumātua who can wow you with the words they use.

For someone my age, you have to really think about what you are going to say. It is easier for old people to get away with things, but a young person really has to prepare for their kōrero. It is a performance.

He spoke in te reo Māori. He started with a mihi to everyone and there were tears flowing down all our faces to hear Pop talking. I was just blown away.

I'm not sure that the speaker can be the judge of his own performance. It is up to the people listening to decide. There are some signs you are doing well — if everyone is still listening, that's good. They are all engaged. They laugh at your jokes. They smile. They murmur in agreement. Even listening is very vocal: 'Āe, kia ora.' If it is a silent, quiet group, you know you need to pull something special out of the box.

If I get to speak at a funeral, it is a performance and I am putting on a show, but it is also the highest honour to be allowed to speak. Oratory and kōrero are the way we honour people. A lot of Pākehā do the same thing by writing books about the person. But we never did that — it is all oratory.

You have to have good memory and recollection. The downside of oratory is that the message can get muddled up when it is sent down the line. What started out as one story is completely different years later. Mary might have had a little lamb originally but by the time you hear about it all she has left is a chop.

I might stand up and say something and another person will follow me and say, 'No, this is what actually happened. My tupuna said this.'

Then another person will speak: 'That is what some people think, but this is what they actually did.'

So there is debate, and that is healthy. In the end, it turns out, after all that, that Mary actually had a cat.

Pākehā's experience of oratory can be different from ours. First of all, they might not understand a word as they sit listening on the marae. That is why I always translate what I say at the same time. But the translation is never quite as good. If they were able to understand the words in te reo Māori, they would be blown away by how beautiful they are.

The way Māori use words to describe things and events is so poetical. Oratory is your time to put all the things you have learnt out on the floor for the public to hear. It is your time to deliver the message in the way you feel right.

One of the things that can be off-putting is the way we deliver the words — like a haka, pulling faces and staunching everyone out. This is a cultural factor. We actually express our love through the haka and the poking of tongues and the aggressive delivery.

If you said these words in English as violently as they sound in Māori, it would be terrible: 'We thank you all for coming!!! To all those who are dead — may you rest in peace!!!'

I steer away from the yelling in my delivery because I am generally in funerals. I like it to come across soft and beautiful.

But once you understand what that gentleman or lady is talking about, it will change your view. When I get Pākehā families walking in now, they are all saying, 'Kia ora, tēnā koe.' They are often doing a te reo Māori class or attending a wānanga to study Māori. I think that is amazing. The number of people taking up classes is wonderful. These people will gain the knowledge that will let them appreciate oratory when they hear it.

That is the beautiful thing about oratory. It keeps our culture alive. It keeps our language in its best form. We are able to recite whakapapa, we are able to share our identities, our stories, our love for another — and our hate, our grief. We are able to tell people what we think of them — whether good or bad. You can do that on the marae, expressed in whichever way you want.

But be prepared for backlash later from your own whānau or from manuhiri kuia.

At a lot of funerals, the floor is opened up for tributes. Some skill at oratory makes this a better experience for everybody. Probably, if you picked an average Māori and an average Pākehā, chances are the Māori person would be more comfortable speaking to a group.

Oratory is important, and not just on the marae. It can start with using te reo Māori at home, when you're having a cup of tea or going up the road. The little points of kōrero all help. We used to say to baby Francis, 'Ka kite,' and he would respond, 'Bye bye.' Now he is up to saying, 'Ta tite.' We are getting there.

The tamariki's first experience doing it might be with karakia. We will ask one of them to bless the food for the whānau. The last time we had Moronai and baby Francis's birthday, instead of me standing up and thanking everyone for coming, we got Nikora to thank them. He did it in English, but that was okay — he had the right words and the right message: 'Thank you for coming to celebrate baby Francis and Moronai's birthday. I want to thank Grandma and Granddad for opening their home to us. Now I'm going to invite Dad to bless the food.'

We have karakia at home in the morning and at night. We get together at least once a week to have prayer and family discussion about what is happening in the coming weeks. All that kōrero needs to be led and every week one of the kids will lead it. This is preparing them for when they will need to stand and speak on the marae.

In my own childhood, learning about these things started at Broadwood Area School.

'We have got manuhiri coming, so there will be a pōwhiri on Thursday. Francis, you are speaking — you tautoko, and Takuwai, you are the next speaker.' You had to do it maybe twice a year, so everyone got a turn.

When we moved on to Hato Petera, we had to speak more often because there were more events to speak at, such as when the school would do performances to raise funds. I loved that. It wasn't just everyday manuhiri. We were going out to fancy hotels and shops to do our karakia and mihi.

I was able to refine my speaking. We were asked to attend when The Warehouse opened branches. That opened up a new world to me because up north we only had one of those. There were so many in Auckland.

Sir Stephen Tindall was on a roll, and he and Pā Tate were good buddies, so a lot of The Warehouse money went into Hato Petera. We got all our beds, blankets and mattresses from there. This was Pā and his networking and relationships.

I learnt a lot about oratory listening to Pā, even following him around The Warehouse branches, because he adapted the church ways and views to suit different situations. We were used to listening to him in the school chapel, but here he was in the middle of a shopping aisle, blessing everything and giving a whakapapa to the lightbulbs and the lamps. It took about two hours to get around all the aisles touching everything.

There was always a hākari at the end, of course — usually a sausage sizzle, but there was more to it than a regular Warehouse sausage sizzle. This was Pā giving out tikanga advice: 'We must end with kai hākari to eliminate the noa.' He could adapt our

Oratory is important on the marae because it does a lot of different jobs.
It is how you learn about what is right or wrong in a public setting.

traditions to anything from the Eucharist in church to blessing underwear and nighties in The Warehouse. It was wonderful.

I still suffer anxiety issues and get nervous when I have to speak to a big group. To get over it, I have to dig deep in my soul. I say to myself: 'Just stop — and go. Kōrero.' As long as I have a couple of points to mention, they will all rise in my mind as I speak.

I have seen lots of public speaking courses that tell you to look at the back of the room and move your eyes across it while you are talking. But I like to look at people. Are they on their phones checking Facebook, or are they getting out lollies? That's no good. I try to find the two or three people in the crowd who look at you when you are speaking and nod along. I will always look back to them as my guides because I know they are engaging with the kōrero.

So deep down, I might be a nervous wreck and I am always very conscious of the situation, but I have to appear to be the calm, collected person who is officiating at the funeral service. It's my job to make sure everyone else is comfortable. 'Please don't be shy — come forward and share your words about the loved one.'

Some are harder than others. Like a funeral I officiated at not so long ago, for a person who was just twenty-three years old and had died by suicide. I had been contacted to do it because the mother had seen *The Casketeers*. I was so nervous. It was very touchy. And they were not Māori. I might have been more comfortable with my own people, when I would have understood better what everyone was feeling. I would have known the boundaries and how far to go. It is not easy to have a celebration of a life in a case like this — it is just very sad. But you have to do what you have to do.

KAIORA

There was no allowance made for nerves in my whānau when I was growing up. Part of the reason I am who I am today is that Dad was very much of the view that when you know there is something wrong or you need to say something, you must speak up. You will never get a better opportunity to express things. If you are in that moment, catch it. Later, you may regret not saying anything.

This is in an open forum. If you are invited to speak, it is just another kaupapa. But sometimes I get there and realise I'm about to talk in front of a lot more people than I was expecting. And it is not being filmed. There will be no editing to make me look better. So I just put my head down and go.

I've never written a speech. I find it boring if people read their words. They sound monotone and I don't sense them connecting with the people.

If I am given a kaupapa to talk about, I will try. I may not stick to it, but there are other things around it I can talk about. I will just say what I want. And generally, those are the best talks, because it is personal and I can relate to individuals. I get disappointed with myself if I don't get the response I'm looking for.

After your speech, you have a waiata and that completes the mihi. My dad didn't like it if you didn't sing a waiata. He put his stick down and hammered the ground with it and that meant you knew you had to sing a song. It's tikanga.

There are still differences between what men and women can do when it comes to oratory. But it is changing.

If everyone is still listening, that's good. They are all engaged. They laugh at your jokes. They smile. They murmur in agreement.

On the marae, at a tangi, you might see wāhine get up and talk on the night before the burial, where there's no tikanga as such. The kaumātua will lay the stick down and get anyone to talk, even tamariki.

Usually, the only time you will see wāhine speak on marae is if they have been invited to. Otherwise, men do all the formal process of welcome and pōwhiri. If a group doesn't have a tāne who can speak for it, women will still be refused, and the hosts will offer to find a tāne to speak for them.

Otherwise, women's kōrero to the marae is in the karanga. That is how we share our message, as our group is walking on.

We are also known to tell the men what to do. I have seen my aunty giving them growlings. She will sit at the back and if something annoys her, she won't stay quiet about it.

If the male forgets certain parts, the wahine will let him know: 'Hey, you forgot to mihi this,' or, 'You have left this out,' or, 'Don't forget you have karakia — Uncle is just here to do the karakia.' They will get really annoyed. Growing up, I've realised it's our duty to tell the men what to do.

I really enjoy listening to my husband speak. Whatever the occasion, he tends to capture people's attention by throwing a laugh in at the right moment. He is always able to make people laugh.

There has only been one time when I noticed he held back from speaking. It was the tangi for an uncle who was a returned serviceman and well known in the iwi. We were there with my mum and there was a lot of my family Francis hadn't met yet.

It was the first time he had been welcomed on this marae. Uncle Hone was there. Uncle Manu was there. There were all these high-profile activist people.

'It is your turn to speak,' I told him. 'They are asking us to talk.'
'No.'
'Mum is waiting for you to talk so we can go.'
'Not now.'
'My gosh — we have been waiting for her so long. I have Baby. I'm tired. Well, you tell me when you're going to go. I'm going to wait outside.'

'What's going on?' said Mum. 'Tell him again. If I have to go over there, I will get angry.'

'You don't want Mum on the taumata with you because everyone will know who's been getting a growling.'

At this point, some of the manuhiri had gone and the room was half empty, so Francis got up and spoke and he was fine. I think it was just nerves, which was unusual.

'Who is this fella?' said Uncle Hone Harawira.

'This is my husband.'

And that is where he met Francis and saw some potential. Not long after that, he invited Francis to read the news on Te Hiku TV up north. Oh my goodness — it was live every morning and it only aired in Kaitāia. There was no autocue, so he had to read it from pieces of paper with one camera looking at him. But he met quite a few people there who are now well known on TV.

TWENTY-ONE

WHAKATAUKĪ

If you have a lot of these in your kete, and you know them all in te reo Māori, you should be able to kōrero in any setting. Stand up, quote your whakataukī and relate it to the people around you.

KAIORA

Our show uses a whakataukī for each person whose tangi is shown. I love them. On the radio station Mai FM, they used to say, 'It's cool to kōrero,' and try to get people to learn a word a day. 'It's cool to kōrero' was almost a whakataukī itself.

On a marae, if anyone gets up to do a speech, they will use a whakataukī. It does the same job as a waiata — it draws a line under the kaupapa of their kōrero and sometimes it sums up the meaning of their speech.

I did a paper on whakataukī at Unitec with Scotty Morrison and learnt so many of them. We got to know them so well that if people in your group said just a few words from a whakataukī you knew what they were talking about.

For example, there is a whakataukī — 'He kanohi hōmiromiro'. Hōmiromiro means 'sharp'. The whakataukī means you have sharp eyes, like your eyes can spot a needle in a haystack.

When I heard other people use 'miromiro', I thought, 'I know that word. It is to do with the sharp eyes.'

Then I used it one time with someone who was very up there in te reo Māori.

'Did you say miromiro?' she asked.

'Uh-oh, what have I done?' I thought to myself.

'What does that mean to you?'

'I've always been taught it means sharp eyed. Pinning something from a distance.'

'Yes, it does — well done. Where did you learn that?'

Thank goodness for Scotty.

My father didn't teach us traditional whakataukī in te reo. He just had lots of little sayings to live by, often in English — such as 'be kind'. And at the end he would say, 'That is your father's whakataukī for today.' He also used a lot of quotes from the Bible as his whakataukī.

People take whakataukī very seriously. The expert who worked on the ones for our last book and the TV series didn't just throw them at us. If there was a certain kaupapa, she would say, 'I think we should do this one instead,' and give us a whole lesson about why it was the right one for that situation.

At that level, a lot of Māori gurus will teach you what something means before you use it. It's not like a jingle that you teach kids.

Lots of iwi have whakataukī that are special to them. Where I'm from there is one that goes, 'He iti pioke nō Rangaunu, he au tōna — Although the pioke fish is small, it may have a big wake behind it.' There are whakataukī for every place I have been to. People will acknowledge their whakataukī and educate everyone who hasn't heard it before. I think that is awesome. When iwi compete at events, they will often have T-shirts with their own whakataukī on them. Some are very ancient; others can be traced back to individual writers.

There is one I know that was said by a rangatira down in Ngāti Kahungunu. 'My strength is not of the single warrior but that of many,' which is, in te reo Māori, 'Ehara taku toa i te toa takitahi, engari he toa takitini.' It refers to the collective effort necessary to succeed and complete tasks.

I shared that one on the Tipene Funerals Facebook page with a photo of all our staff. We were taking photos because we are so proud of our staff and we had everyone together for once. As soon as I saw that photo, I thought of that whakataukī. I thought, 'Wow, look at our whānau.' People also share it when they graduate. It refers to them having their tūpuna with them on their journey and acknowledging their ancestors.

Our team is awesome. Our backgrounds are so diverse — Tongan, Niuean, a couple of Pākehā even — and when they are put together we can do great things.

Mary the embalmer, who is Pākehā, joined a week or two after the photo was taken and had been put on social media. She came up to me after it had gone out on Facebook.

'I was just wondering if there is a chance I could be part of the group photo,' she said. Unfortunately, she had to wait until the next group photo.

Another whakataukī I ought to mention is: 'He rā whawhati te kō — It's a day to get things done.' Around the time I met Francis, I would wake up saying that.

'What are you saying?' he asked.

I tried to explain. It talks about having a spade and it being a day to use it to get things done.

'No, this is a day for bed, thank you,' said Francis and put the blanket over his head. 'Tell Scotty he can keep his whakataukī to himself.'

I'm envious of people who know a lot of whakataukī. If you have a lot of them in your kete, and you know them all in te reo Māori, you should be able to kōrero in any setting, if someone asks you. Stand up, quote your whakataukī and relate it to the people around you.

FRANCIS

One of the main reasons we have whakataukī in the show is that they have always been a big part of our lives. A key one was: 'Seek for the highest that you can, and if you bow, bow to a lofty mountain — Whāia te iti Kahurangi, ki te tūohu koe me he maunga teitei.' That meant that I was going to try my best to do something, and if I didn't fully succeed, it would only be because I had come up against the biggest obstacle of all.

Whakataukī are instilled in a lot of people. There was one example at the New Zealand Television Awards when a Māori actor named Jayden Daniels won best supporting actor. He got up and started his kōrero with the well-known whakataukī mentioned above, about success being a team effort, but he only got halfway through it. I don't know if he got flustered or overwhelmed but it didn't matter because all the Māori in the room finished it for him.

'My strength is not of the single warrior but that of many — Ehara taku toa i te toa takitahi, engari he toa takitini.'

I use that whakataukī a lot. It speaks to humility. And it acknowledges there are lots of driving forces behind any success. We wouldn't be here without support from a lot of people. Jayden wouldn't have finished his whakataukī without support from a lot of people either. That was a moving moment. We were united and we supported him.

The whakataukī I know I acquired mainly at school. They were a huge part of growing up and we learnt them from some great teachers. There was a lady up north who was our principal at the time, Whaea Pani Hauraki. Another was Mr Gregory, who we always called 'Sir'.

All of these people had a huge influence on our speech-making. We learnt to mihimihi at school. All these whakataukī were written on a board or given to us in a booklet, and when we stood to do our speech-making, it was important to start with a whakataukī. It would set the tone for the kōrero.

At an awards night or school prize-giving, we would start with the one Jayden Daniels used. It has to be appropriate to the ceremony and set the tone. Whatever the kaupapa was, the whakataukī had to come first. That is how they got embedded in our minds.

When I was at a tangi for a teacher who died, I caught up with some mates from school who I hadn't seen for years. We were having kōrero and joking around and pretty soon we were quoting to each other the whakataukī we had learnt back in those days. We are in all sorts of walks of life now. Some have done well. Some have not done so well. But we had all these whakataukī in common still.

One we shared was 'Kua tika a hē — What was wrong is right.' It is acknowledging that things change and what was not tolerated once can become acceptable over time. In this case, we were referring to the impact of Covid and how you could have a funeral and not harirū as a part of it.

There are many things about tangi that are done differently now, compared to just a short time ago. That has us bringing out that whakataukī a lot. It is very relevant when you are talking about not having a kai hākari after the tangi. Sometimes we have it before the tangi because people are so busy and need to get away as soon as it is over.

How can we lift the tapu before we have even started the sacred ceremony? I don't really know the answer, except to say, 'What was wrong is right.' And the kaumātua will reply, 'If our ancestors were here today, they would be unhappy.' That's true.

I appreciate our kaumātua for their leadership. There will be a time when that responsibility falls on our shoulders. We will be making the same complaint to the next generation, and they will be telling us to move with the times.

Whakataukī are like a lot of things in life — everyone sees them slightly differently. Someone thinks that an apple is mainly red, another person thinks it is mainly green. But you do have to back up what you say in your whakataukī. You can't just say it and sit down.

But it is all part of the art of oratory. It's supposed to be spontaneous — done on your feet and off the top of your head. So you have to think really quickly.

And if you don't know about the plant or bird that is part of the poetry of the whakataukī, you are in trouble. For instance, there is a whakataukī whose second part is very well known, though not its first. 'Hutia te rito o te harakeke, kei hea te kōmako e kō?

Māku e kī atu, ki a koe. He aha te mea nui o te ao? He tāngata, he tāngata, he tāngata!'

It starts off talking about the seed of the harakeke. You have to rip it back to let out the new life that comes through. And it finishes by saying that the greatest thing of all is people. I struggled with that. I can see what it is talking about, but what does the harakeke have to do with people?

The explanation is that you see the little things and, then all of a sudden, they start to grow. Ka pai. I can relate that to the birth of a person. And harakeke are hard to kill off or pull out of the ground.

Another favourite of mine is: 'Ka mate kāinga tahi, ka ora kāinga rua — If there is a problem at the first home, the second one will be fine.' That is what it means. Always have a Plan B. It is saying that if my son and I are having a massive fight and he is not listening, I will send him to his grandparents. That is kāinga rua. They will sort the problem out. Grandparents seem to have a better way of dealing with things. The whakataukī is not about the homes, it is about the power of the grandparents.

The same saying could be applied in other ways, to anything where one thing isn't working but another might — perhaps a child is not doing well at their school but they will thrive at a different one.

One of the whakataukī we often use at a tangi is: 'Ko ngā rārangi maunga tū te ao tū te pō, ko te rārangi tangata ngaro noa, ngaro noa, ngaro noa — The lines of mountains will remain standing forever, but the lines of humans will disappear, disappear, disappear.' It makes the point that people are only here for a short time compared to the rest of the natural world. But it can also be interpreted another way. The lines of mountains can symbolise lines of knowledge — lines of whakapapa that will remain after we die. It is also a challenge. It is up to us to pass on the knowledge so the culture doesn't disappear like the people, but that it survives like the mountains.

TWENTY-TWO

WAIATA

*Waiata have so many functions — at hui, pōwhiri, karakia, tangi.
Nothing is complete without a song.*

KAIORA

Waiata have so many functions — at hui, pōwhiri, karakia, tangi. Nothing is complete without a song. Whenever you see someone talk on a marae, a waiata always follows. Some kaumātua say any kōrero doesn't mean much if there is no waiata to support it. Waiata gives it mana. And it has to be the right waiata for the kōrero.

I keep this in mind today if I sing a waiata with Francis at a tangi. He looks around before he finishes his kōrero and I know it is a sign for me to get up. I am mindful of his kōrero, and what songs are right. Sometimes, I get frustrated if I haven't been able to choose the song. I might not want to sing 'Pōkarekare Ana'; I might not feel it is appropriate. I might want to sing 'Toro Mai'.

But the fact is you can never go wrong with 'Pōkare': it is a favourite and it is beautiful and everyone knows it, so you know they will join in. You can make it relate to the person who has passed away by changing from 'e hine' for a female to 'e tama' for a male.

At the funeral home, we sing 'Whakaaria Mai' a lot. Even though it is one of the most famous hīmene, I don't expect our staff to know all the words. But it is cool if, when we sing hīmene for whānau, our colleagues do come in and join us.

I was always taught that if someone is singing a song and you know it, you should join in. Don't just stand there, be a part of what is going on. You are on the marae to be together with other people, so sing together with them, too.

You always have to be prepared. We had Whaea Norma at the home for a service before she was to be taken back to Kaitāia. The family said they wanted to have a farewell for her in Auckland before she headed up north to go home.

But I didn't know one of her kids was a kaiako on staff at Māngere kura kaupapa and the other was a principal at a school up north. Our little chapel was packed.

They had told me they would have things sorted because they knew the tikanga. They wouldn't need Francis to do anything. That was great.

Francis was about to head off to the Henderson branch when one of the whānau stopped me: 'Sis, I know I said we don't need him to do the karakia but whānau are struggling because there are so many people here. They will struggle, so is it possible for Francis to do it?' I had to call him back.

'What song am I going to sing?'

We knew they already had a hīmene chosen but I told Francis if he was being asked to do this at short notice, he should be able

When Dad went to the marae, he would always go with someone who could sing. Usually it was my mum. She was always there, next to him or behind him. She always knew what to sing.

to do whatever he wanted. And, of course, he sang 'Whakaaria Mai' to open and 'He Hōnore' to finish.

I watched the whānau as he started to sing and when they began crying, I knew that was a sign he had done his job. Then when everyone else started to join in, that was a beautiful feeling, too. When it came time to close the lid, the family said they could take over from there. A good fifteen or twenty of them came up the front, playing the song and making a powerful noise behind me.

This is another thing about how waiata works. I didn't know the words to this particular song and it annoyed me. I am used to knowing the words so I can be singing when they place the lid on the casket and be in that moment with them. I could feel the beautiful harmonies behind me but I couldn't join in properly. I had to hum instead.

As we transferred Aunty from the chapel to the hearse, they started a hīmene I knew and I was so pleased that now I could join in. That is an example of how waiata can work to help with healing, when it brings the emotion out.

There are so many beautiful waiata. We should learn more of them. There are so many kinds, too.

There are some that may have old lyrics put to tunes that have been composed more recently. A CD came out some time ago called *Te Hononga*, which has some old waiata from Te Tai Tokerau that I love.

There is a lament called 'Rimurimu' that is special to me. The song relates to a mother who lost her child and went to the seaside to sing for him. I had heard it at a graveside performed by an aunty. I didn't know all the lyrics; I just thought it was very beautiful when I heard it performed.

I sang it once when I was pregnant. I probably wouldn't have been allowed to if I had checked with anyone. But Francis and I had been invited to speak at the World Indigenous Business Forum in Rotorua in 2018, when I was pregnant with baby Francis. We spoke about tikanga and how it relates to us in our mahi and how it had been a benefit for us.

At the end, I sung this lament. Then one of my aunties said, 'Baby, do you think it was a good idea that you performed that particular waiata while you're hapū?'

'What would be the difference if I performed any other waiata?'

'It just feels different because it is for a mother who lost a child.'

'I am in a workspace that deals with this every day.'

But it made me think I should be a little bit more careful with my song choices, and that what a waiata is about is important. But the same time, I felt I had some mana and since I was the one carrying the baby, I could perform anything I wanted. I was very strong with this view. You can get underestimated when you are pregnant. I don't like that.

Many waiata are attached to specific places and every iwi has their anthem. I am from up north and Ngāi Takoto on one side. There is a song I sing from there which is special to us. I had to sing it for Uncle Hone Harawira once at a Ngāpuhi dinner. I didn't know he would be there until it started. I was down the back and didn't even know if he could see me. As he finished his speech, he said, 'Now I am going to invite my niece and she is going to come up and sing my song.'

Dammit. I looked at Francis.

'He didn't say my name — just yours, baby,' he said. 'Get up there.'

I was walking up thinking: What song should I sing? You only have a few seconds to decide. Then one came to mind that everyone from up north would know. It is called 'Ko Mātou Tēnei ko Ngāi Takoto'. Uncle Hone joined in. It is nice when you get up if you can sing a song you both know, especially if it is because you are from the same place. And yes, you can always sing 'Pōkare', but if you do, a lot of people will be thinking: 'Oh, that's boring — she couldn't even think of a song.'

Another time, in another setting, Uncle Hone called us both up and I just got Francis to do it. It wasn't a Māori song; it was a Pākehā song. I was like, 'Nah — I'm not singing it. You can do it this time.'

I know Pākehā worry about being at some occasion where they are expected to sing the waiata to conclude a kōrero. Well, there are Māori who can't sing, too, believe it or not. I have seen a person who couldn't sing do a dance instead. I thought: 'That's different. Really different. Too different.' I have seen some people share a poem and then I think: 'Didn't they just talk and now they are talking again?' I think it's better to sing badly than to recite a poem. But at least the poem can be a bit like a whakataukī — it has a message at the end. I didn't hear any message at the end of the dance.

There are other things you can do, if you can't sing. Usually, you get other people to help. 'Is there anyone here who would like to sing my song?' I feel terrible for them, but within seconds there will be someone there. You see them shuffle up to join them. I have done that for a few people and Francis will always do that.

At home, when we have karakia we always have hīmene, too. The kids are all different: Nihaka gets shy, Mikae will sing. Baby Francis can do a haka. He likes to do that.

But the person in our whānau who loves waiata the most is big Francis. Every night he can, he will play the guitar and sing while Nikora plays the drums. Sometimes it sounds just like you are at the pub.

One night, I was cooking muttonbirds, which doesn't make Francis very happy, but maybe the music distracted him from the smell. They were having their little play on the guitar and bongo, singing hymns, while I was snacking away on the muttonbird. Those are moments we treasure.

There is a bar that has live music near us. Francis has asked if he and Nikora can go down there and play a few songs, so they are practising for that. They sounded so good, I asked if they could just stay home and play for me, and then I wouldn't have to put up with the pub noise.

Francis's dream is to perform the national anthem at an All Blacks game. I said I would try to make it happen. I would definitely buy a ticket to see that.

When I was a child, I had to sing the waiata after my dad spoke on the marae. He taught me to sing a song that related to the kōrero. It wouldn't necessarily have been right to sing 'Whakaaria mai' or some other hīmene as a waiata tautoko.

Dad played the guitar and taught us a lot of famous Te Tai Tokerau songs. He insisted we all knew what waiata we were going to do before we went on the marae. We would be in the van together driving there and he would say, 'What song are we singing?' Sometimes we sang Mormon hymns or other songs in English.

Uncle Mike was an incredible man. He composed a waiata that contains our whole pepeha. It talks about our family's maunga and so on. It's all there — our whakapapa, identity and language. It's beautiful.

When Dad went to the marae, he would always go with someone who could sing. Sometimes, that meant my sister and I got taken out of school so we could be with him. But usually it was my mum. She was always there, next to him or behind him. It was just his thing: 'I need my wife by me.' She always knew what to sing.

It was our role to stand by him the whole time, listening to his kōrero just so we could support it at the end. I would think he was finished and be ready to sing, but he would signal to me with his stick, meaning, 'You can't go anywhere. Dad is going to talk again.' Sometimes, it was hours before we were allowed out of the wharenui.

The people in the kitchen tried to feed us: 'Uncle, are you hungry? Manuhiri, have something to eat.'

'No, I need to stay here.'

'Your girls might be hungry.'

'No, they are all right.'

We were not all right. We were so hungry. We could see our cousins playing outside. They came and asked us to play but we had to say no. It was torture.

If we were lucky, an elderly aunty would come along and give us a lolly and override Dad. 'Hani, your girls are hungry. I'm taking them in the kitchen.'

It wasn't just one or two marae, either. We visited a lot of marae all over the north. The good bit was all the things we got to see. We witnessed amazing kōrero. We saw aunties and uncles challenging each other. We saw them Bible-bashing each other.

'Oh Hani, are you coming here to preach this? We don't need to hear that.'

'I just finished karakia and I acknowledged your karakia. Acknowledge what I have to say today.'

It was interesting if an aunty got up to speak. Was she allowed to talk today? If she got up, it often meant she was growling someone.

Even when people came to our home, we had jobs to do. I thought we had seen enough of these people on the marae, but here they were again a few days later, having a good chat with Dad. And we were not allowed to play inside while they were having a kōrero.

We were supposed to know what to do. Get them a cup of tea. If we didn't bring a biscuit too, Dad would give us a nudge.

'Mum, Dad says they need a biscuit.'

'We don't have any — take them some bread.'

I am so grateful for what I learnt in these ways. And all within the space of ten years. Now my sisters ring me up to find out what to do if they are going on a marae. Whether they are allowed to speak, what they should sing — and I am able to tell them, thanks to the work my dad put in with me.

FRANCIS

Our family, like many whānau, has waiata that are special to us. Some are very old, some are not so old. Our Uncle Mike Tipene was the leader of the whānau at one time, and he and the other aunties and uncles had waiata, te reo Māori and haka classes. Those waiata were taught to them, and thankfully our aunties and uncles wrote them down. When we had family gatherings or wānanga, we were taught them in our turn. It was another way in which the identity is being kept through mōteatea or chants. That is a blessing.

They were not your typical aunties and uncles. They did so much. At that time, they would have been our age, working at their day jobs with not a lot of time to go to classes. They had kids to raise, kai to prepare. The fact they did what they did and stuck with it makes me respect them enormously. But I didn't even realise they had this side to them and that their culture was so deep within them, not until they started teaching us.

Uncle Mike was an incredible man — a social worker, an athlete and someone with a lot of knowledge that he used humbly. He composed a waiata that contains our whole pepeha. It talks about our family's maunga and so on. It's all there — our whakapapa, identity and language. It's beautiful.

It was his foresight to see what this waiata could do. When we first heard it, all we heard was the tune and the beat. Now we understand there is a whole lesson in these two minutes. It makes us very proud to have this in our whānau. No other whānau can use it. It is a taonga that will last for many generations to come.

When someone like Uncle Mike departs this life, these are the greatest gifts they can leave behind — more than material things. They define us.

I only met him once, but he lives on through all the stories that people tell. A lot of people knew him. You just mention his name and they start to share stories straight away.

His grandson, my cousin Mike Tipene, is just like our grandfather. He is the one who leads our family now in waiata and haka at gatherings. These things have been passed down to mokopuna who probably weren't very interested at that time. Young Mike might have just been hanging around but he absorbed it all without realising it, and now he is passing it all onto us and I am so grateful.

TWENTY-THREE

KAPA HAKA

There are times in kapa haka when you get to shine and be an individual, but kapa means a group and togetherness. That is the beautiful thing about kapa haka.

KAIORA

Kapa haka has been important to me my whole life. I love the feeling of performing. I love the build-up before you get on stage, the feeling of having all of my tūpuna behind me. You have spent all this time working towards this moment — giving up weekends, taking time away from your whānau — all to spend twenty or forty minutes on stage. It is just a beautiful feeling.

My dad was right behind it. Performing was a duty as far as he was concerned. There was no room for being shy. I took to it straight away. He told me to get up, do my piece, then sit down again, and I did without thinking about it. It was no big deal. Partly, I was doing it so I would be allowed to go outside and play. Do the mahi, get the treats.

My cousin Missy Edwards was part of Te Waka Huia, which was and is one of the top groups. Dad had a lot of respect for these guys because they were the champions. He encouraged us to go and learn Whaea Missy's songs. So we got to learn the waiata she was learning with her group.

From a young age, we were picking up the poi and swinging away like adults. My group won the intermediate schools regional competition one year.

After that, Missy taught me at college. She was very active in education in the north. My Aunty Matilda, Uncle Hone and Aunty Hilda formed a kura kaupapa in Kaitāia. It was one of the very first, and Missy came down to be our tutor.

She taught us a lot about taonga. We learnt to sing about the mate — our tūpuna who had gone on ahead and paved the way for us.

The first year Missy taught us, we won the regionals against a Bay of Islands school. The following year, we were in the nationals. We were all excited about our song because the entrance had a powerful mihi that was about tino rangatiratanga. Our kaitātaki tane, the male leader, unravelled a tino rangatiratanga flag and started waving it.

He called to us to stand and uplift one another and encourage what true tino rangatiratanga means. The feeling I got was so awesome.

I was like: 'Wow — where did that come from?' I hadn't seen this until the actual performance. We had seen him practising with a stick, not the flag. I had to work to keep my focus and do my bit properly.

We didn't come anywhere in the nationals. Full-immersion schools won first, second and third places.

When we got back home, we were on an absolute high from

representing our school and doing what we thought was such a good performance. Our parents were waiting. We were proud because we thought they were there to acknowledge us.

But no.

They pushed our tutors into a room and there was a heated discussion. Mum took us home straight away, so I didn't know what was going on, but another night at practice the parents turned up again.

'Do you know what they are talking about?' asked my friend.

'Maybe doing a fundraiser?'

'No, they are pissed off we used the flag at the nationals,' she said.

'Why is she pissed off about that?'

'I don't know.'

'It's what we've been singing all the time.'

Maybe the tutors should have told the parents what was going to happen rather than let them find out later. Using the flag was a very strong statement and we were representing everyone back home, so it reflected on them. Perhaps some more transparency would have helped. But none of the tutors got fired.

I got to join Te Waka Huia in 2003. I couldn't believe I was going to be in my all-time favourite kapa haka group. It was so exciting to be part of it. When you know the nationals are coming up, you watch the calendar and count the days.

The groups practise for six months solid. They write the songs, learn the words and come up with the choreography. Then the top forty in the group are picked to do the actual performance.

During the competitions, you watch all the other groups closely and soak it all up.

When you go to school the next day, almost all your mates know all the words to their favourites. If you didn't know the words, you felt left out. I couldn't understand how someone could know all the words to almost every song.

I tried out for the Te Waka Huia team to compete in the 2009 nationals and got selected. The group performed in Tauranga and won that year. I didn't get to go on stage with them, but I was one of the two reserves. They can only choose forty performers and there was an excess of maybe fifteen wāhine. For me just to be one of the reserves was an honour. I was still proud to be that much a part of it.

They never close the door on their performers, so even now I could go back and perform for the group if I wanted to. Some people go and come back, but I've never gone to another group.

I get envious if I see some new groups forming, especially up home. I feel a call to go north and be part of them, but that is a lot of commitment and a long way to go.

Some people are willing to do that — travel a long way to be part of the groups. That is how strong the passion for kapa haka is. It has grown into a huge movement and a massive competition. People are fiercely committed to it. They might live in Auckland but drive hours to be part of the Te Whānau-ā-Apanui team and do it every weekend.

And it is expensive. There is petrol to pay for, time off work for some people, wānanga fees, your uniform. It is not just about getting up and singing and dancing.

When I told Te Waka Huia that my tāne and I were starting our own tangihanga funeral home and that it would be awesome if they could come to the opening, my tutors and kapa haka whānau

Kapa haka has been important to me my whole life. I love the feeling of performing. I love the build-up before you get on stage, the feeling of having all of my tūpuna behind me.

were all excited and couldn't wait for us to start our venture. I will never forget the teachings of Ngapo and Pimia Wehi.

* * *

I was always taught to acknowledge the person who created the waiata. If you are going to sing a song, you should know who wrote it and where it is from. That is a tikanga.

Songs can become very popular through being done in kapa haka. They spread like crazy. After a performance, everyone will be talking: 'Did you hear that?'

If it is a subject that is dear to the people, even though it's on the radio, you will hear people singing it wherever you go. In the street. At a pōwhiri. That will inspire you to learn it and then it becomes even more popular. If the tune is catchy, then it is easy to learn the lyrics. It will probably have been put on YouTube by someone. If you haven't already learnt the song, you will feel left out.

When I met my husband, he was playing his guitar and knew some of the waiata I knew. In fact, he was singing a song from Te Waka Huia. It had a very catchy tune and was very popular. Everywhere you went, you sang it if you knew it. And my husband knew it. When he started singing it, it got me hooked into him.

But when I joined in, he didn't like me singing with him.

'You know, you don't have to sing all the time, too,' he said.

And just when I thought I really liked him. I thought he had a real problem. But then he started chasing me.

FRANCIS

One of the things kapa haka did for me was teach me a lot of discipline. Sure, Nan and Pop taught me discipline at home, but this was different because it was about being disciplined in a group. It taught me patience. It taught me sometimes you have to work with other people who might not work the same as you. Sometimes you can be an individual, but most importantly it is discipline.

The first lessons in kapa haka probably happen at church, when you are made to do things in unison — sing, find harmony, hit a note. We learn to sing as a group, not as individuals. There are times in kapa haka when you get to shine and be an individual, but kapa means a group and togetherness. That is the beautiful thing about kapa haka.

But it is also about learning how to be competitive. Up north, it was more of a festival than a competition. It only got competitive when I moved to Auckland. People say you are just out there to have a good time and that it isn't about winning. Oooh, but it is.

I didn't take to it at first. It seemed to be just standing in a line and being yelled at. 'Ki raro, hope.' Hands down. Hands on hips. Go to the beat. It annoyed me. Why weren't we doing more important things, like practising singing and haka? There were lots of frustrating moments. I was the guitarist and I would have to strum the guitar for thirty minutes straight, making sure everyone stomped their foot on the beat. Hands up. Hands down.

Even though it is a team thing, there are definitely stars and they take any chance to show what they can do. Being in the group gives you an extra boost of confidence. There were lots of moments where I was given special roles, and to this day I am so

It was about being disciplined in a group. It taught me patience. It taught me sometimes you have to work with other people who might not work the same as you.

grateful. They have been a platform for life. To be honest, I really wanted to stand out, and being in a group was quite annoying.

It is good for some kids not to be shoved out the front. A lot of them are shy and don't like that side of it, although they like the singing and dancing. It's important not to pick individuals out too quickly. Put the shy kids in the second row, so they can get used to being on stage with a bit of cover. If they ever forget the words or moves, or get overwhelmed, it will be okay. They can watch the person in front for the actions.

But years later, when I was tutoring, I found myself doing the same thing that I had hated doing, with the kids I was teaching. 'Hands down. Hands up. Go to the beat.' You have to do that, because those are the foundations of moving together.

Later, we were taught the different beats, how to speed the guitar up and slow it down, do a waltz beat, make sure they kept up.

Now we go to my kids' school and teach kapa haka to Nikora and Moronai and their classmates. I am happy to do that. A lot of kapa haka that is taught at the schools is done off YouTube. They don't have the qualified teachers, so they push play instead.

I was shocked when I saw that and probably a bit quick to judge. It was just that there was no one there who knew how to teach them. It blew me away to learn that they had no one to play the guitar and tell the kids, 'Hands up. Hands down.' But YouTube was better than no kapa haka at all.

When my wife and I went along with the guitar and got the kids hyped up, spread them out and helped them with their moves, it was really exciting. It was like the difference between performing with a DJ and dancing with a band. The energy was great. Having live people with a real instrument makes them so much more enthusiastic in their performance. I wanted to make sure my kids and their classmates got the same things we did, so we put them through the same drills.

Another big thing about kapa haka is that it teaches you a lot about te reo Māori. In order to do a winning performance, we had to understand what we were singing. We would be taught the song, then get the explanation. It was wonderful. It wasn't just singing and being physical and running around the stage. It was also about knowing what the singing and chanting and stomping about meant.

That made it a lot more real to us. A lot of the songs were about things that were important in our whakapapa — ancestors or rivers or mountains. A lot of them were beautiful tribute songs to people who had passed away. These helped bring out a lot of emotion.

Or they were waiata about what was happening at the time. Around then, we were going through a rough patch up north with fights over using 1080. We sang a lot about conservation, ngahere and protecting Tāne Mahuta.

Songs are being written all the time. Ancient pieces are still performed but there aren't many and most people know them. We can't keep doing them or people will lose interest. The Tūhoe people are wonderful — they have their own haka that every group must perform.

Every group does their part slightly differently, with a different energy or at different speeds. Some are angry, some sad. Some are telling a story, some spreading a message. The haka, poi, and entrance and exit song can all be adapted. Some people take props on stage, anything from drums to kites.

Every group will have a traditional song. Some will use traditional instruments, such as the kōauau and different flutes that are very beautiful. Not everyone can play these, so they really capture your attention.

Kapa haka has even taught me lessons I use at work as a funeral director. When there are cases where grief is strong, people may speak words that are inappropriate or rude, but that is grief. Then you have to be a team player and just accept — well, that is their way of dealing with it. Just like I learnt to strum the guitar the same for half an hour, now I find I can let people have half an hour to cry before an arrangement. I have learnt to be patient and it gets easier as life goes on. In my twenties, I was all about bang bang bang, let's just do it. It took a while for the kapa haka lesson to sink in — you have to adjust to moving at the same speed as other people. Sometimes you have to let others set the pace.

TWENTY-FOUR

TĀNE AND WĀHINE

A visit to a marae doesn't begin with a man doing a haka. It begins with the karanga by a woman. That is the first call, the haere mai. The woman's voice is the first. That is a role of a wahine.

KAIORA

My mother always taught us girls that in the home setting our place is meant to be looking after the kids, cleaning the house and cooking the food, and that it is for the males to work. Women need to rear the children and teach them what they need to know.

That was kind of nice, but times change. I don't really believe in that now.

Every now and then, my mum will come around and watch me doing what I do. Then the questions start.

'When is the last time you stayed home for three days straight? When is the last time you had quality time with your kids?'

Oh, Mum — thank you for that. We have had a few debates along these lines. In her mind, she has always been a mum, and that is the woman's role. But she is starting to realise it is different now. She is learning, after sixteen years, that our mahi is our bread and butter and that it is something Francis and I do together. It is not typical work. It is a privilege to be in the industry we are in.

She has backed off a lot. But she will always be around to say, 'Hey, come on, be a mum now.' If I get home and dinner is not ready, I get: 'Do you think you should leave work earlier?' It's a nice idea but it's not realistic. I do have days where I feel guilty because dinner is not ready and we are relying on Uber Eats or chicken nuggets from the freezer. I know they are not made with love, although my boys love them.

My sisters would agree more with our mum, even though they have lives like mine. The reality is that two people have to work to provide a comfortable life for kids, nowadays. We can't just have one person going to work.

But my parents expected us girls to grow up, get married and look after a home and babies. They gave us piggy banks and encouraged us to save.

I wasn't even expecting to be a mum, especially of five boys. But they are a blessing. They all have their needs and the bigger two are becoming independent. Sometimes people will comment that I really need to have a girl.

I get disappointed when I hear that. The pressure of not having a girl is already on me. I don't need other people to remind me. I can count. And I can accept the beautiful children God has given me. Someone once said to me: 'Plenty of people have a boy and a girl. Not many people have five boys.'

And they are learning to be good men, not just in traditional roles but as nurturers. The older ones look after the little ones. The little ones don't like being bossed around by the big ones but they put up with it. And everyone is working together. The boys know when we are busy and they have to help out. It's such a normal part of my life that I don't really think about it until someone asks: 'What is it like having five boys?'

I'm not sure how different things would be if I had a girl. I do know Francis would be head over heels for her and our household and our work would definitely come second. He would agree to anything she said.

At work, I don't like it when I come up against males who assume females can't manage a business. I do not like to be underestimated and I do not like when people assume things about what I can or can't do. People even assume the male has to be the one who is the funeral director. Even among our staff, the division is about 50:50.

'Where is Francis, please? I believe he is the manager,' said a man who walked in off the street one day. He's not the only one to have done this. They can't have watched the show very closely or they wouldn't be making this mistake.

'Francis is one of the managers,' I tell these people, 'but he is not here now. How can I help you?'

I am the person they need to talk to if it is about financial decisions, whether it is a new industrial-strength vacuum cleaner or something a lot bigger.

They end up talking to me when I explain how we split up our duties. But until then, if the two of us are there, they will just address all their remarks to Francis.

Finally, he will say, 'This is my wife. She makes the financial decisions. You can talk to her.'

And, of course, I get a bit annoyed he has to use the wife thing.

That is a role of a wahine — she is the giver of life and the first voice we hear in life. Her role is to welcome the people.

Francis is better about his spending now. He will tell me if he is considering buying something. It's been a while since he ran off and made a purchase.

Even though Māori tradition defines roles between men and women quite conservatively, they also recognise the important part each sex has to play. My dad almost never went to a marae without our mum. He missed her and felt incomplete if she wasn't there.

If there is no wahine on the spot to do a karanga when you get to the marae, you have a problem. But you never saw a male do a karanga on the marae. That was for women only. There is a male reply to the karanga that is used sometimes called a takutaku.

When we took my Aunty Chrissie back onto the marae for her tangi, I asked if one of my other aunties from the marae could do a karanga for us. I was told she couldn't that day because she had some sort of sickness.

We were there on the manuhiri side to say our final goodbyes. Would we have to go on without a karanga? We started to move forward and had got halfway and still no one had responded. Then I heard one of the male cousins start a takutaku. I was cool with that.

Normally Aunty Chrissie would have been the one to do it. Some of her children knew how to karanga but they couldn't that day, because they were in grief, too. I was really proud of our cousin for doing the takutaku.

Even though the roles are strictly separate, for something involving kawa, if there is a bit missing you can always find a way to make it work and get there in the end. You don't give up altogether because there is a bit missing.

When I was working for Peeni Henare, I went on a marae with a group of people. Nanaia Mahuta, who is a cousin of mine, was one of them, and the kaumātua invited her to sit at the front by the men. It was his marae. This was long before she was made Minister of Foreign Affairs.

On the other side, the tangata whenua got up and growled us for having her at the front.

She stood up and sang a waiata as she walked back to the women's area. It was her way to acknowledge it wasn't her decision to sit there. Then, from our group, the late Rudy Taylor got up and said, 'No, we have had many women sit up here — Helen Clark, Titewhai Harawira. Many prominent wāhine.'

He was going hard at the tangata whenua. He made it strong. 'Don't you move,' he told Nanaia. But they didn't feel welcome. Rudy was very angry about the whole thing.

FRANCIS
A visit to a marae doesn't begin with a man doing a haka. It begins with the karanga by a woman. That is the first call, the haere mai. There is a reason why the roles for men and women are split up on the marae. If you don't hear that reo from the woman, you are not going anywhere.

We are all standing there, ready to go on. When that cry of welcome in joy or sadness is thrown out across the ātea of the marae, that is the signal we are starting kaupapa. All the people are ready to do the haka, but if you don't hear that voice, you stay still.

The occasion might be a birthday or wedding. We might have been to the church first then come to the marae for a reception.

Times are definitely changing. I have seen women speak at Waitangi. I'm a practical person, and it is what it is. You have to welcome guests somehow, so whoever can speak should speak. I like that we are able to change.

It might be a tangi, and we might be holding a coffin, which is very heavy.

When we get to the marae, we are starting again. When the woman throws out her voice, it is so beautiful. You could say that when you are born, the first thing you hear is your mother's voice from the pushing, pain and joy when you come out of the womb. And when we come onto a marae, it is the voice of a mother we hear. It is symbolic of that — the woman's voice is the first. That is a role of a wahine — she is the giver of life and first voice we hear in life. Her role is to welcome the people.

And straight away, so many things come into your mind. They are happy thoughts most of the time, sad thoughts sometimes. You might be reminded of earlier tangi when you brought a grandparent or parent onto the marae.

Inside the wharenui, the role of the male is to stand and speak. He welcomes guests. Up north, we acknowledge our elders. We have had many great kaumātua and orators, such as Nick Adams and Dodi Tipene. People don't know they always have women behind them somewhere. Even a great orator can bugger up sometimes, and when he does those women will come at him: 'Why the hell did you say that? That was stupid.'

So when the men are talking, they know not to go too far off track, because if they do the wāhine will have no problem saying, 'You shouldn't have said that. Go and apologise.' It's the same as what happens with a husband and wife.

In the past, karakia was generally led by a male. Now, with different churches having female ministers, it can be a man or a woman. It doesn't matter so much as long as you have a leader.

If you look at Kīngi Tūheitia, every time he has an ordination, there are female ministers present and it is a lovely balance.

These rules about what men do and what women do are tikanga, not kawa. They can be different for different iwi.

Some years ago, we heard a lot on the news about MPs wanting to speak on the marae when they were not supposed to. A famous case was that of Helen Clark when she was prime minister.

It shouldn't have been such a big issue. Women can speak on the marae, just not in the formal setting. At the start, there is a way to do things. Then you finish the exchange of kōrero, have a hongi, then you can sit down and will be invited to talk. I think there was a miscommunication in that case.

We have to be realistic, as we are with other customs that we are adapting to the changing world. In Pawarenga, we have females who stand and greet visitors because we are running low on kaumātua. Our old men are dying, so our kuia are getting up to do the mihimihi. Before they speak, they will say something like, 'Ehara tēnei i te takahi i te mana o te tāne, ahakoa ka mau panikoti ahau engari kāhore ngā tāne ki konei — This is not to diminish your mana, because I am a woman. We just don't have anyone available who is a man.'

Times are definitely changing. I have seen women speak at Waitangi. I'm a practical person, and it is what it is. You have to welcome guests somehow, so whoever can speak should speak. I like that we are able to change.

Having monuments like headstones is relatively new in terms of tikanga. When it is time for the unveiling ceremony at the gravesite, the women will normally go up in the early hours of the morning to the grave and cover it with a korowai before the sun comes up. They will take off the plastic that has been protecting the headstone and decorate the grave. That is a beautiful thing wāhine do. That is not a very strict tikanga. The men are probably too busy getting kai ready. If there were only men around, then we would do it.

It is normally the women's job to put up the photos of the loved one. They will know the lines of connection and the whakapapa and put the pictures in the right order. Sometimes, a kaumātua will come along and say, 'No, that photo at the top should be in the second row down,' and explain what the connections are that need to be acknowledged.

TWENTY-FIVE

TAMARIKI

There is a lot to learn. You can't always force these things on kids, but we hope at least they are getting the feeling from watching their parents that what we do is about something important.

FRANCIS

There are so many challenges for parents these days. When I was growing up with Nana and Pop, we didn't have much and things were simpler. I didn't know what I was missing out on. When they said we were going to the marae, it was as though they had said we were going to Rainbow's End. All the whānau would be there and I got to have time with my cousins. If it was for a tangi, I got to look at the casket and the dead body.

Recently, my aunty died up north.

'Aunty has died,' I said to Nikora, our eldest. 'Do you want to come?'

'Where is it?'

'Pawarenga.'

'Oh, no.'

They're not really into it. Sometimes I feel like just putting them in the car and taking them. It is good for them to do things like this. These are not opportunities everyone gets. There is a lot to learn. You can't always force these things on kids, but I hope at least they are getting the feeling from watching their mother and me that what we do is about something important.

Funerals are like a university, where we go to learn so much about life as well as the reality of death and dying. You hear amazing stories about people's experiences. You hear about what's good to do in life. You are exposed to your language and culture. I learn something new from every funeral I do.

I haven't told them there is wi-fi in Pawarenga and everyone uses cellphones now. Just when I thought we would get away from all that.

Of all our boys, so far the one who seems most connected to his culture is Moronai, the second oldest. I think he would like to follow me into the business, too. He loves all things Māori. Sometimes we are having a good kōrero, but then a cousin pops up on his phone and he is off. Children are so easily distracted, and no wonder with all they have to distract them. But deep down in his heart he is a true-blue Māori.

Nikora, the eldest, also has a good grounding in his culture and te reo Māori. Some things he does surprise even me and also tell me he was listening when he was younger.

One day at work, he was with me when I had a hot chocolate in my hand. On the way to the office, we went past the dressing room. I went in there, said good morning to the tūpāpaku, and he said, 'Dad — your drink.' And I thought it was wonderful that he remembered the tikanga even when I had forgotten. And I put my drink outside.

He has been singing a lot of hymns on the guitar. I never thought he would be into hymns. Some of them are well-known ones that I have always sung and that he had gone off because they have been thrashed. But he is very talented musically and, in order to make himself interested, he reggaed them up and it sounded neat. That is progress — when a young person takes something old and changes it into something else. It keeps them interested and keeps it alive. It's using the past to make the future.

There are two things happening there: he is learning a hymn and he is making it more appealing so it will stay around longer. His mother started tapping her foot and I thought, 'We would never have tapped our feet to this music before.'

All the little correcting we did with him is paying off. He even had the words in te reo Māori without having been sat down and taught them.

So now we have a tikanga at home in which, if Dad grabs the guitar, Nikora will jump on his guitar too. It's not a compulsory tikanga. We don't have to do it every night. But we know we can if we need to have a sing-song after a busy day or an argument.

We were invited to a Labour Party launch, to be part of the presentation, and I got him to come with us.

'Mum and I need you to play guitar for us. We are entertaining this crowd. There will be quite a lot of people. And the prime minister will be there, too.'

'I can't. I can't do it, Dad.'

'Yes, you can.'

We had a few nights of practising. He wanted to do his song with the reggae beat and that brought a spirit of excitement to the event, which was what it needed. He played and everyone sang. It was uplifting.

When I was growing up with Nana and Pop, we didn't have much and things were simpler.
I didn't know what I was missing out on. When they said we were going to the marae, it was as though they had said we were going to Rainbow's End.

'That was a great opportunity for you,' I said afterwards. 'Not everyone could have done that.'

'I know, Dad. Oh my gosh.'

He couldn't believe he had done it. It was a great confidence boost.

* * *

One night, I was lying on the couch watching the TV news with the kids. The six-year-old came over for a hug and I noticed he was putting on weight. I didn't say anything about it. Then I noticed the seven-year-old was also getting a bit chubby. I started to think about our eating and whether we should be doing a better job of choosing healthy food for our children.

We were in lockdown and everybody had put on a bit of weight, but I realised the kids weren't being very active either, so I needed to implement a tikanga in my home to make sure we take care of their physical needs.

'We need to do something about the tamariki,' I said to my wife. 'We were never this big when we were young.'

It wasn't really about how big they were. It was about how much I had seen change in such a short time.

'Yes, I know,' said Kaiora. 'Look — the six-year-old is able to wear the eight-year-old's clothes.'

I realised our lifestyle was terrible for them.

'What do you think if, after school, the kids have to go outside and play? We usually get home about 5:30, so they can play till 6:30.'

They weren't used to that sort of routine, but we discussed it with Maggie, who stays with us and helps to look after them all the times we aren't there. She was very pleased. I get the impression they don't do much activity at school. They just use the swings to sit down and talk about TikTok.

I told the kids we would start by playing tag.

'What?'

'Look what we've done,' I thought.

We can't blame the kids. It's not their fault they don't know what tag is. I explained that you count to ten and then run and try to catch someone, and when you do, they have to count to ten and catch someone, and so on. We started playing and everyone was huffing and puffing, getting red and sweating, and it felt really good.

When we stopped: 'Dad, that was cool. Can we have our phones back now?' They always revert to the phones.

'No — no phone until the big hand gets to eight, then you can have half an hour.'

We are trying to limit phone use during the week, with a bit more allowed on the weekend. At 7:30, they were sitting right by me waiting for 8 o'clock.

'Is it time yet?'

'Not yet.'

Now we have our priorities sorted at home. If it is a rainy day and we can't go outside for exercise, we will adapt.

The kawa of the home hasn't changed. We have the same rules about shoes inside, when you wash and how you eat. But we have some new tikanga as well, which is fundamental in our children's lives.

Our children are used to te reo Māori but they are not bilingual. For lots of different reasons. They have attended a variety of schools. Nikora and Moronai were taught by Madeleine Sami's

That is progress — when a young person takes something old and changes it into something else. It keeps them interested and keeps it alive. It's using the past to make the future.

mother. Mrs Sami was the te reo Māori teacher and very staunch on all aspects of reo and tikanga. Moronai was in a bilingual unit at his intermediate school but that didn't seem to suit him. Nikora has a te reo Māori unit at his school but it is not compulsory.

Our oldest two were kura kaupapa children until year six, then they went to mainstream schools because I wanted that balance. As long as they had the foundation in te reo Māori, I was happy.

It might be good for everybody if schools were more consistent in how they approach tikanga, so that everybody could understand each other better when they leave school.

Our big boys have lost a little of their reo since they finished primary school, but they still understand a lot. My wife and I like to kōhimuhimu, which means to whisper but also to talk behind someone's back. When the kids are around and we want to talk about them, we use te reo Māori and their ears always prick up. I forget they have the foundation.

I try to get them to converse with me in te reo Māori. They can't quite piece sentences together but I know the words are there, which is very humbling to me. Maybe we could have done better and got the Pākehā education implemented some other way.

For baby Francis and the other younger two, their te reo Māori is even less than that. When they hear my wife and I speaking, they laugh and make jokes between themselves and make fun of the way we talk. That's our fault for not treasuring that.

We need to kōrero more at home. Like the kids, we spend a lot of time on our phones, talking in English. Our kōrero in the home leaves a lot to be desired, but we are trying to bring them up right in so many ways.

TWENTY-SIX

RONGOĀ

Ancient medicine is accessible and has much to offer us today, used alongside modern medical procedures. Health is a vital issue for our people.

KAIORA

Māori traditional healing is making a comeback in some areas and with some people. We have to do something, because Māori have so many special health problems.

My dad was a sick man in his later years. He was in so much pain. He was deteriorating quickly. His skin colour changed. I probably had more of a relationship with him then because I was the one who had to do a lot of the looking after. My siblings were jealous that I had days off school because Dad wanted me with him. But he liked having me because I listened to him.

I remember so clearly, looking at this purple-black thing that was supposed to be his leg. His toe got a scab on it that wouldn't go away. Then it got amputated and he couldn't walk properly. He had to learn how to walk without a big toe. Mum thought it was funny, but he didn't.

He was very staunch in his religion and his hāhi, his Mormon faith. He would ask for healing blessings from his friends. He went all over the north trying to find someone or something to give him some relief from his pain.

Once, we went to see some sort of faith healer. It was in a college hall and it was packed. He was standing up the front with a mic. I wasn't used to this form of healing. I'd never seen anything like it.

'Is there someone on this side suffering in the legs and in the arms and in the stomach?' the healer asked the room.

Dad was on his feet straight away. 'Yes, it's me. Please heal me.'

I was sinking into my seat. I knew this wasn't right.

'It is someone who has come from a long way away.'

Dad was gutted — he didn't fit that description.

Then we heard about someone in Huntly who could help, so we went all the way down there from Kaitāia — Dad, my brother and me travelled down to see this person who had taught my dad and my mum about rongoā Māori, Māori medicine. He mixed it with spiritual healing. He used plants like matipo, kūmarahou and kawakawa to make his own medicines.

We were in Huntly with people I didn't know and I was really uncomfortable. Dad was getting involved in all sorts of things because he wanted to heal. He believed this rongoā Māori was going to kill all the germs he had. All the diabetes and other ailments would be gone.

He tried to convince himself that these things were doing good and he was getting better, but if they ever helped it wasn't for very long. He was all about getting that quick fix and believed tradition would help him. Maybe they did help him live a little longer — I don't know how you'd be able to tell that.

There was also a lot of karakia involved in Huntly. Every morning, a tohunga came in and did a karakia over Dad's body. After that, he would feel heaps better in his mind and in his body. It would help him just for that moment, whatever it was.

We made lots of this medicine and took it back up north. But by time we got back to Kaitāia, he wanted more of it. Mum spent a lot of time boiling up plants and making his concoctions. In the morning, there were all these milk bottles labelled matipo juice or kawakawa juice or kūmarahou. They all looked like dirt to us kids. He had to have them morning and night; a bottle a day, if possible.

When it came time for the school sports, he told me I would win my race if I tried some of this stuff. I tried some one day. It was so foul that I never tried it again. I might give it a go again now. I see things like kawakawa balm around. It would definitely be a lot better if you didn't have to drink it.

But because my dad believed in this medicine so strongly, he would try to force it on me when I was sick, but it caused more vomiting than anything.

'Dad, are you sure you are giving me the right stuff for the sickness?'

He got very frustrated with me. 'Drink it if you want to get better.' And if it didn't work, he tried to find something else for me to take. I was like a guinea pig for his experiments.

It was kind of sad but I know it was him showing his love. He thought he had found something good and he wanted to share it with me.

He probably did himself more good when he cut out all the fizzies he used to drink. He had a really bad thing for Coke.

Every time he would massage Dad it was like he was giving him life. He had karakia every time he pushed somewhere. I think he must have said a prayer for every part of his body.

If there was no Coke in the fridge, he would get really angry and go into withdrawal. But he cut out a lot of bad food and drink, and that probably did as much as the medicines to help him live a little longer.

It wasn't all bad. Once, I went with Dad to Ngāwhā, where one of the locals was a healer in massaging. Not everyone was allowed to go in and you usually had to go without a spouse or anyone, but because I was the only one there with my dad I had to go in with him. This person started with karakia, then pretty much every time he would massage Dad, it was like he was giving him life. He had karakia every time he pushed somewhere. I think he must have said a prayer for every part of his body. My dad came away feeling so good that he slept the whole night for the first time in ages, and my mum was so impressed she went to the masseur the next day.

I love and respect those who practise rongoā Māori and make it their own to help the living. For those who are no longer with us, at the funeral home, we use some natural treatments, such as kawakawa leaves. I first saw them being used on a TV show. A Taranaki family wrapped the body in leaves and then woven flax to help preserve it. It might be a good option if you don't want to use embalming. It is believed to help preserve the body, but you must use lots of it and it must be in direct contact with the skin.

In the rest of my family, I have one sister who really believes in traditional approaches. As for me, my midwife when I was first hapū with Nikora preferred to use only natural or homeopathic forms of medicine, instead of paracetamol or other commercial products.

I didn't mind at the start, but there were times when I got chronically sick and her stuff wasn't working, and that's when I ended up in hospital. I thought: 'This lady — what is she doing to me?'

I think the most important thing with health is to use what works.

FRANCIS
Nan and Pop boiled up water with kawakawa leaves and used it for everything. If you fell over or cut yourself or hurt something, you had to bathe in the juice. Everything was about these leaves. You had to find the leaves and use them to make a potion. It had a really nice clean smell. I was so young, I never bothered to ask them what it was. I just knew that was the fix.

Nowadays, you can just go and buy kawakawa cream at the shop and people use it for all sorts of things. But it was not so available in the old days. I remember Nan ringing around looking for it. If someone had it, we hopped in the car to go and get it.

Generally, in Pawarenga, the kuia and kaumātua would use traditional healing for the older people, but the rest of us would get taken to the doctor.

But best of all — don't get sick or hurt yourself, because in the country there was no chemist just up the road. If the ambulance came, that was a big deal. You thought, 'Oh gosh, who is it?'

Then you got on the phone for a kōrero. Back then, it was a party line, so every time it rang, anyone in town could pick it up and listen. You were supposed to wait for your particular ring. I remember Nan talking for ages and it was only after I left home that I realised it wasn't private. But it meant that once one

Nan and Pop boiled up water with kawakawa leaves and used it for everything. If you fell over or cut yourself or hurt something, you had to bathe in the juice.

person found out why the ambulance had come, everyone knew within moments.

We didn't have tonics or supplements of vitamin C to take. We just had a cup of tea for any occasion — morning, noon and night. A cup of tea to wake up. A cup of tea to go to school. A cup of tea when you got home.

Nan and Pop were lucky in their health. Nan still is, and I feel so blessed that she is still with us. Pop had good health until his eighties, when he started to go downhill. That was a good innings for him.

I probably should take better care of my own health. You'd think I'd be more conscious of it being in my profession, but I really only go to the doctor when I'm sick. Every time I get someone who has died from a cancer, I think we should get screened, because people so often say how a given person would still be alive but they caught the cancer too late.

But that is how I think I am going to die — of cancer. I have no special reason to think that, I just do. I don't smoke or spend a lot of time out in the sun. I don't have any risk factors at all, really. And usually, in my family, people die of heart attacks.

When it comes to dying itself — not just the bit that happens afterwards, which is my job — I love our new legislation about voluntary euthanasia. Sometimes, when I pick up tūpāpaku and see the state of their bodies, I can see what it must have been like for them in those last moments of life, when they were helpless and suffering so much. I hope their ascension into Heaven is worth all the suffering.

I trust the legislation. It's not going to encourage suicidal people to kill themselves. It's going to let people end their pain.

There is a lot of paperwork to be done and a lot of safeguards have been put in place. There are many guidelines there to be taken into consideration before permission can be given.

This is not in line with tikanga, but my wife and I still support it. I think it is hard for outsiders to judge. You have to be the person who is involved in the middle of that situation and enduring the pain in order to understand it.

My wife and I get annoyed when people say funeral homes were in favour of the law because it is good for business. That is ridiculous. In the long run, the same number of people are going to die — 100 per cent of them. It is not a business opportunity.

TWENTY-SEVEN

DEATH AND DYING

We are here now in the human world, Te Ao Mārama, and there is just a veil separating us from the other side. If we go through the veil, all our ancestors and other people are there.

FRANCIS

My understanding of dying and what happens throughout is based in Māori beliefs. In a lot of kōrero, you will hear matua referring to 'ki tua o te aria — beyond the veil'. We are here now in the human world, Te Ao Mārama, and there is just a veil separating us from the other side. If we go through the veil, all our ancestors and other people are there. We are living side by side with this thin veil between us.

We can talk to the people on the other side. At the grave or cremation, they are being committed to Hawaiki-nui, or to Heaven or whatever else you might want to call it. There is a fine line that keeps each of us on our own side. We are here and they are there. I imagine it as a beautiful, billowing white veil. They can see us, even if we can't see them.

Māori tell people when they are dying, 'Haere rā, haere rā.' We are saying, 'Go there, to that other side.'

Exactly where one side ends and the other begins, I don't know.

That is one of the reasons tangihanga is so important. We always talk about it helping the living, but it helps the mate as well. When we have our final send-off with clergy, or our own personal payer, that prayer is a send-off prayer, to make sure they definitely do get through the veil.

Sometimes, if things aren't done right or we haven't followed tikanga or had proper karakia, maybe our loved ones are poking through the veil. They haven't been able to get all the way over yet. Otherwise, they can be stuck between both and turn a little bit pōrangi. This is why funerals are so tapu — because you are between the worlds. The part of the ceremony where the body is committed definitely sees a transition to the other side of the veil.

We have a name for those who have not been able to get through the veil properly — ghosts. If they seem unfriendly and act out a bit, it is because they are upset and frustrated at being stuck here. And until the tangi is complete, they have to be here. When I am at work at 2 a.m., I try not to think about who is in the building with me that I cannot see. But they are real. My wife and I have little prayers of our own to keep us safe. I have to remind myself that I chose this life.

Here we are, going about our business with the tūpāpaku hovering around. We don't want to get on their bad side. We have to be respectful. Hopefully we will commit them properly and get them over.

Sometimes, things can happen that are unsettling. I used to try and pretend they weren't, but they were. If we sense the mate is really unhappy, we will get a priest to come in and say a prayer to help settle them temporarily.

For instance, when I am handling the body, I might say something bad. If I bring the trolley out and am half asleep and the wheel doesn't click down properly, I blame the mate: 'Damn. They are so heavy.'

The tūpāpaku will put me in my place by making me hit my head. That's my punishment. I am like a kid being taught that my actions have consequences and I need to think about what I have done.

So we always act towards the person like they are alive. We don't say silly or inappropriate things. And if I knew the person, which I often do, I will kōrero to them: 'Okay, that's fine. Sorry, Aunty.'

When I go to Pawarenga, I will visit Pop in the cemetery and we will have a talk. Last time I went I thought about how the people on the other side could be looking out for me because I was so nice to them on their way over. It should work both ways.

I try to get my staff to share my attitude about respecting the dead while they are still in the funeral home, and the living when they come in, too. Once, we had a whānau in to do a dressing in the dressing room and the young boys were outside cleaning the cars and listening to their radio. It wasn't super loud. They were just doing what boys do, but I told them off anyway.

'Turn that radio off. There's a family in there.' It didn't feel right. The whānau probably didn't even notice the noise but showing that respect mattered to me.

Another part of the process that is very beautiful is what happens at Cape Rēinga. It is always very special to me when I

We always act towards the person like they are alive. We don't say silly or inappropriate things. And if I knew the person, which I often do, I will kōrero to them: 'Okay, that's fine. Sorry, Aunty.'

go there, to the place where the spirits leap off and leave the land behind on their final journey to the other realm.

Even at the tangi, in Auckland or wherever, we acknowledge this by saying: 'May you go in peace and safety as you begin your journey from Te Rerenga Wairua, that place where spirits dive into the ocean.'

The first time I went to the Cape, I just wanted to look for that cliff and tree and the spot where the spirits jump off. I had heard about it so many times from my kaumātua. I would have been about ten that first time, on a trip with the convent school from Pawarenga. The teachers explained it beautifully.

Later, I took the family and showed them and told them the whole story. I was pleased they were interested. I might not have told the story as well as it had been told to me. It didn't go too smoothly.

I told them how when we die, we go to the spirits' 'waiting room', where we are waiting for God to see us. That is the traditional church belief, too. Then I added in the jumping off.

I guess for the kids it was a bit confusing, hearing it for the first time. Then I confused myself. You don't really think about things till the kids start asking you to explain them. Then you have to really think hard. But at the end of the day, we got to the nitty-gritty and somehow it all made sense.

There are different beliefs but they have the important parts in common. It is like a map — here we are and here is the place we all want to end up, but different people, or religions, have different ideas about which routes to follow to get there. It's like when we use Google Maps and choose which kind of transport we are going to take.

TWENTY-EIGHT

THE MEDIA

We are very conscious of the platform we have and the need to use it carefully. But we will use it.

FRANCIS

Because we are on TV, people think Kaiora and I represent our people. We are supposed to be typical. We are not. But we are ordinary. As we said at the start of this book, we can only live our own lives the best way we can, in line with what we have been taught and what we want for our whānau.

We are not statistics to be used to prove a point.

I get whakamā at the portrayal of Māori in the media. I always get upset to see us shown in a bad light. It makes me so sad. When we had the very first episode of our show, so many Pākehā came up to me and said: 'It's good to see Māori doing well. Good to see Māori in a positive light.'

'Thank you so much,' I said, but I was angry because I knew what they meant, that it was *unusual* to see Māori in a positive light. And they were right. It was unusual for them. But not for us — we have always seen Māori in a positive light.

I asked my wife, 'Are they going to say that about the people on *The Block*?'

I don't want to sound like a sad person. It is great that now we have had the fourth season, fewer people think it is so unusual anymore. People are used to the show and seeing Māori who aren't some stereotype.

In the early days, it was quite nice that people wanted to meet us. It was nice to get that approval. If they went to the shop near to our premises for something, they would pop in to us to say hello.

'I tell everyone I go to the shop next door to the funeral home and I know the Māori couple Kaiora and Francis.' And in my mind, I am going: 'Oh my God — here we go,' but out of my mouth I am saying, 'Thank you, thank you, thank you.'

Then you see something bad in the paper about P or children who are not being looked after properly. I often just scroll past those stories. I don't need another sad case to bring me down. I like to read positive things. But I don't want to hide the fact we have problems because we do.

The potential we have as a people to do well is unlimited, but we are all raised differently and we all come out differently.

People say Māori have come to this because we are cut off from our spiritual connections. But there are lots of people — Pākehā and Māori — who aren't spiritual but don't commit crimes or treat their children badly.

The real problem is not being raised by loving parents. That is all we really need. Religion is important but people don't turn evil if they don't have it. They need to learn good habits. They need to budget a bit better. If they are going to have lots of partners and kids, they must be prepared to work hard for their children.

The other aspect of the media that my wife and I have to deal with a lot is being asked for our views on anything to do with Māori. It really is a privilege that people think that what we have to say might be worth hearing. I am grateful people trust us enough to ask us. It is never a hōhā.

But oh my goodness, how the media work! They will ring at ten in the morning and say, 'Can we interview you in half an hour?', when I am at work and about to do a funeral. Or they just ring up and say, 'Can we do an interview?'

'Okay. Happy to help.'

'Great — can you come to the studio at 5:30 in the morning to do a pre-record?'

'No, thank you. Try another funeral home.' I don't need any more reasons to get up at 5:30 than I already have with my kids and people dying at inconvenient times.

One time, we got interviewed for our thoughts about the council thinking of burying people standing up. What is that like in regard to tikanga and what were my thoughts? That was a bit different. I had to think quickly and managed to make an analogy with the fact that we say rest in peace, which makes me think we should be lying down. My view was that you can't rest standing up. Thank you for asking.

Both my wife and I believe it is important to share our knowledge. Our staff are very knowledgeable on tikanga and other subjects and they could answer many of the questions we get asked, but the fact is we are the front people so we end up doing it.

When we say anything in the media, we have to think about the big picture. We know not everyone agrees with everything we say.

I get whakamā at the portrayal of Māori in the media. I always get upset to see us shown in a bad light. It makes me so sad.

And it is a balancing act with our business. A lot of people might love us, but a lot of people also might hate us if they don't like what they are hearing. I would rather be quiet and just get on with my job of looking after families but it isn't an option anymore.

And I know every time I express an opinion, there is someone sitting at home watching and saying: 'He is so wrong. They are not going to take my body there.' I know we will lose business but sometimes you just have to say it the way it is. So we do.

This book is an example of that, too. I hope we have made it clear that these are our points of view. We are not saying this is what anyone apart from ourselves should think or believe. If people do, that's great. But we don't expect them to or insist that they do.

KAIORA
I feel we have an obligation to comment in the media if we are asked to. During the pandemic, there has been a lot of struggling and sadness around tangi and the rules for gatherings. A lot of people asked us for guidance. We talked a lot about that in the media and also in the book *The Covid Chronicles*.

With a lot of iwi, I couldn't give them any answers because I didn't know their tikanga. They wanted examples of safe processes so they could take their loved ones home or transfer them between regions.

We had to be so careful about what advice we gave because we could become seen as 'real' advisers, when we were really just people with a bit of knowledge and some opinions. We didn't want to be seen as official spokespeople for anyone — not our industry or our whānau, our hapū or our iwi.

THE MEDIA

But it would have been wrong to say nothing. There was so much bad stuff happening.

I didn't feel we were getting anywhere with my local MP when we were trying to find out what would be permitted when we went from Alert Level 3 to Alert Level 2.

When we were about to change, everyone knew we would be allowed to have gatherings of up to 100 people and this relieved so much pain for people who had lost a loved one in the middle of all this. But then we went back down and were suddenly told you could only have ten. I could not believe it. If you had a family with a widow and six children, then partners and mokopuna and brothers and sisters of the mate — sometimes even the parents of the loved one — would not be able to attend their tangi.

I felt we needed to make a statement and not just get angry and react like my activist family up north would. I had to be careful. People think I am this lovely person they see on TV. I am that person, but there needs to be a way to tell people if I think something is wrong and I am angry about it. So I put a video up on social media saying how upset I was — not for me but for the grieving families. I was trying to be a voice for them, because they can't reach the sort of audience I have been given.

It was also about me and my grief at not being able to do my job, but mainly I was just sick of seeing families upset or missing a true send-off and having things changed on them without any warning.

There were so many shares of that post. Even my cousin Nanaia Mahuta who is a cabinet minister commented on it in support. People got behind it and told me to keep doing what I was doing.

I know every time I express an opinion, there is someone sitting at home watching and saying: 'He is so wrong. They are not going to take my body there.' I know we will lose business but sometimes you just have to say it the way it is.

But it didn't seem to change anything. I had called out to the prime minister but I never heard from her.

Then, in the following days, we heard from Minister of Health David Clark and we were invited to take part in a discussion with him and other people in the industry and the health sector about what we could do.

Even though I always have to be careful what I say and what I post, I was glad to find out I had enough influence to get us a hearing with the government. I am very conscious of the platform we have and the need to use it carefully. But we will use it.

We have not joined the Funeral Directors Association of New Zealand because I think we can be more influential if we stay independent. We have also not stood for Parliament — oh my goodness! — as has been suggested to us. An MP told me she thought we should stand. I said I thought we were more effective doing what we are doing, and she laughed. Sort of.

TWENTY-NINE

TAUIWI

Anything people do to share cultures is usually good as long as it is done with respect. If it is disrespectful, we are totally opposed.

KAIORA

I can count five Pākehā I've met who have embraced Māoritanga and feel connected although they have no blood.

When I was a student, there was someone in one of my courses who was Pākehā and blew me away with how much te reo Māori she knew and how much respect she had for our culture. Near the end of the course, she came up and spoke to me.

'Kaiora, I'm going through an identity crisis,' she said. 'At heart, I feel I am Māori but I have no blood connection whatsoever.'

'Do you not acknowledge your parents and where they came from?'

'Yeah, I do, but I find their ways haven't been the best for me.'

'Why is that?'

'Because I haven't been able to connect properly with people. I've found while learning about te reo Māori that it's not just saying it to someone; it's about everything — where they have come from and so on.'

'Surely Pākehā can do that.'

'No, it's a different feeling.'

'Okay, so how would you like me to help you?'

Then she surprised me some more. 'Well, I haven't had the experience of going to a tangi.'

I thought: 'Okay, how am I going to work this out?'

'I suppose the next tangi in my family you can come.'

As part of our course, we had stayed on a marae and done a lot of basic things. This woman could karanga and did it beautifully. But she wanted to go to a tangi. I wasn't able to do that for her at the time, but she did have a visit to a marae where the experience seemed to be a good one for her.

I didn't want to disrespect her feelings. I can't tell her she can't wear the markings of my tūpuna. You can't say that to an individual. They could be doing it as a form of respect, too, if they have embraced the culture. But if they are just doing it to be cool, then I will have a different view.

I could relate to her, but it is a struggle to work with some Pākehā. I would like to give them an understanding of what whakapapa means. I'd like to try to connect them with where they are from. Surely there is a mountain where they used to live and a home where they have been brought up? And if they are from, say, Mt Roskill, maybe they can be a bit flasher about it in their pepeha and refer to is as Puketāpapa.

I love how much some of our Pākehā friends are embracing our culture in all parts of life, not just getting a moko and saying kia ora. One day, I filled in for Francis at a Pākehā funeral. I didn't know what to expect. When I got to the house, they asked me inside to share a karakia and hīmene with their loved one before we went to the crematorium. They were all Pākehā.

In the case of our funeral director friend from earlier in this book, who was part-Māori and missing out on Māori funerals in his area because people didn't know he was tangata whenua, I offered to help get a mihi sorted that he could put on Facebook.

'Really? You would help me?'

'Of course I would. Let people know you have whakapapa.'

'Is it wrong that all of a sudden I should become Māori?'

That was a tough question. Then we started talking about him having a moko. He thought many people would say he was wrong to get one.

And I am still confused about some of this. I think it should be someone's right to do that if they can whakapapa to it, but at the same time I have reservations.

I've always been in support of any individual's right to believe in what they believe in. I think it comes down to what you feel and how you connect.

My husband and I agree that anything people do to share cultures is usually good as long as it is done with respect. If it is disrespectful, we are totally opposed. It depends how the culture is portrayed and used. For instance, if they are ignorant about pronunciation, I will speak up. But if there is a sense that they are trying and you know they are, then you should show some patience.

I see a lot of Pākehā doing their best to incorporate te reo Māori where they can. Businesses can use it to their advantage. Sometimes when I am shopping, it is the Indian shopkeeper who says 'kia ora' to me. It's nice to get a kia ora back. It blows me away.

People are trying a lot harder. The local school asks us to go in and assist with tikanga. Work colleagues try to do their best with te reo Māori. Ordinary people come in off the street and ask if their spelling is correct: 'Can you just tell me if I have written this out correctly?'

One had written down a famous whakataukī they wanted to use. They wanted to be very specific and I was able to show them where the macrons should go. I thought that was lovely.

A lot of people come back and ask for advice for wording on a headstone. If I don't know, I can still try to help. I will go to Scotty and Stacey Morrison's books for guidance. It is so good that people ask and try to get it right, so we need to help them.

My dad would be so amazed by these changes, especially with Pākehā. He would be encouraging and be proud of what Francis and I have achieved in terms of the funeral home. He wouldn't care about the TV show so much. He would think it was a lot of blathering on about nothing. But he would really appreciate what we do and the use of tikanga in the funeral home, and how it is incorporated in people's final farewells, whether Māori or non-Māori.

FRANCIS
We have been talking for a long time about how Pākehā are adopting Māori funeral practices to give them a better grieving process. But I think we could learn a few good lessons from Pākehā.

For instance, eating after a tangi to lift the tapu. You don't need to pig out. I love the way Pākehā families do refreshments after the funerals. It is not about a massive kai and needing a sleep. Pākehā don't always have a feast. They have a cup of tea and a biscuit or asparagus roll or sausage roll. That is sufficient to take care of the kawa and lifting the tapu.

The important thing, really, is the chance to catch up and talk to each other. Many reception lounges don't have lots of chairs. They are designed so people will stand and move around from person to person to enjoy fellowship and reminisce. They're not there for the kai.

I also love how on time Pākehā always are. You can always gauge how long you will be at the funeral for. One hour. If it is at 12 p.m., you know you will be back to the office by 1:30. I can do another arrangement at 2 o'clock.

If we have four or five funerals on, people might have to wait a little while for you to get to their one. Pākehā understand, but Māori don't like that. 'Are you telling me I have to wait for Mum another day? No, I need her to come home now.' They want to start the process straight away.

I also love how some Pākehā come dressed and wearing make-up. It's very beautiful when they cry. They bring out their tissues and gently wipe their eyes. Not us — we just tangi and pour it out and we don't care what we look like. We would never wear a fancy hat.

For Māori funerals, it is traditionally three days out of our lives for a tangi. But I respect how for Pākehā, when there is a bereavement, the family still carry on with life. They keep going to work and school.

Some people say this is rude, but we still have bills to pay and a life to live. The electricity company doesn't stop charging when

People are trying a lot harder. The local school asks us to go in and assist with tikanga. Work colleagues try to do their best with te reo Māori. Ordinary people come in off the street and ask if their spelling is correct.

someone dies. In most cases, when I am planning a funeral with a Pākehā, the day and time depends on when they can get off work. This one has his exams, so he can't do it. Our niece has just started a new job so we should give her a couple of days to get settled in before she takes time off for a funeral.

A lot of times at tangi, our Pākehā families have travelled to be there just for the day. A hey and hello and a hug and then away again. They have the one-hour service, a cup of tea and disperse back to life. It means the world to the immediate family that people have come. But imagine if they came the night before and sat together around the casket with a wine. Having a drink is not a Māori thing, but it could be a Pākehā thing. A few extra hours for catching up and storytelling could make a big difference.

People talk about death being natural and a part of life, but Pākehā seem to take that a bit more seriously. They say death is going to fit into life. It ends one life, but we have to acknowledge that the other lives will still go on and we work like that.

I get to see both sides and I can see the good in both. Viewing times will be arranged for outside school hours so education isn't interrupted. 'Let the children go to school and we will come and see Nana at four.' I won't judge either side, but I do love the Pākehā way of organising things around work, because this is life.

When we have a tangi, we don't need 300 people there for three days. We should continue to go to work and provide for whānau. And after work, we can go to the marae and have our time together then.

Māori are already at the bottom of the socio-economic ladder, and when a tangi comes we have more days off and put ourselves even further behind. People might read this and say I am turning on my people. I am not. Our culture is important and will survive, but we have to have some limits about how we tangi. Families might have four funerals in a year. That is about two weeks of their time. Normal bereavement leave is three days, and you have to be an immediate whānau member. So a lot of people are having to take annual leave or leave without pay to do what they see as their duty.

Taking on some of the Pākehā attitude to death will benefit Māori because it won't interfere so much with their work and income. You often hear people say, 'Oh, he's always off at a tangi.' It stops people getting taken on. Is a boss going to employ the person who's going to shoot through for a week every time someone dies, or the person who will take off an afternoon to go to a funeral?

I do this in my own funeral home. I don't employ people who are closely related to each other because, one day, there was a tangi and half the staff were gone because they were all connected to that person. I wasn't angry with them. They had to go, and I would have attended the funeral, too. But people don't stop dying and the business needs to keep going.

Each culture expresses things differently. Pākehā express it all on the day of the funeral. It's all out and over. We take four or five days. By the time the funeral is finished, all those tears have run dry. It is not as painful as doing it all in one day. For Pākehā, there is sometimes grief that lingers and is hard to shift because things have been done so quickly.

A lot of Pākehā families have memorial services, without the tūpāpaku present. Before I did this work, I thought that was strange – just having a gathering with a photo. I know it is like kawe mate, but in that case there has been a tangi earlier with the tūpāpaku present. As time has gone by, I've gotten used to it. Especially with uncertainty over Covid-19, it is the way to go for a lot of people.

Often it is the person's wish not to have any official funeral. 'Just put me in a box and burn me. I don't want a funeral.' But the family have needs too for saying goodbye. A memorial service means they maintain their integrity — it follows the person's wishes, but also lets the family have a process.

Sometimes when people want the body taken straight away from the house and cremated without anyone present, I say, 'Why don't I pick Mum up tomorrow morning? Why don't you have a couple of wines with Mum at home tonight? Get some friends and family round and we will pick her up in the morning and have the cremation then.'

They are often so happy. 'That is perfect. We didn't know we could do that.'

We are a service business and will always do what people want. But, this way, we are following their wishes and using our experience to share some possibilities and they are grateful.

They didn't have to have a funeral that they didn't want anyway. They had a nice glass of wine. Maybe a lot of glasses of wine. And that is their funeral.

Māori whānau, on the other hand, never want to lose sight of that body. If it is being embalmed in our mortuary, we will be outside the door, waiting.

I also think we should have a look at our practice of doing things communally. Even the decision about where to bury someone can be a group one. And when it comes to catering and organising a tangi, it is all done communally. Everyone turns up to help and that is a beautiful thing.

But, once again, it means half the family is gone for the morning and afternoon and maybe the night before to prepare the food, do the cooking, serve it and clean up again at the end. It's to save money, of course. We can't afford caterers. You don't want to go into debt to feed everyone. But this is the time we should be getting together and enjoying one another.

If we were all able to eat together, it would be amazing, but that doesn't happen. It is always the same aunties and uncles in the kitchen doing the kai. They will swear black and blue that's what they want, and that is kei te pai. But I wonder if they are missing out while everyone else is having a good time.

On the plus side, the bonding that takes place in the kitchen when preparing food with the whānau is huge. You hear stories and gossip you will remember for a lifetime. You laugh. You get to talk about whakapapa.

If you go to a marae, go into the kitchen and grab a tea towel, you will always be welcome and included. That is how I have met lots of whānau I didn't know well. Peeling carrots and washing spuds, you get to talk about life. There is a bonding in that. That's how we connect on a deeper level.

Imagine if Pākehā families prepared their own food. The stories and the bonding that would be taking place would be wonderful. On both sides, we can see how things could work differently and a bit better.

When I have a Pākehā arrangement to do, I always second-guess myself because I want to make especially sure we do everything right for them. My nerves are always way up there.

I know mistakes will happen but if people ask first, there won't be as many mistakes, and it matters that it comes from a good place in their heart.

They do present challenges. Often, they are more emotionally needy.

An arrangement that would take half an hour with a Māori family could take three with a Pākehā family. There is lots of talking and sharing and listening. They want to go into all the details then. They will want to learn about what technology you have available. PowerPoint shows are getting flash. Floral creations are getting more elaborate. Most families have standard casket sprays but a European family might want one with veges from the garden and some side arrangements. It's beautiful and it pushes our learning.

We also need to be clearer with our Māori families talking about money — from the start and across the board. We are upfront about costs with our families — Māori and non-Māori — right from the initial phone call. We have had complaints that this is insensitive. Yes, it is.

I know the feeling. I had a taste of my own cup of tea when I saw a new hearse and rang up to enquire about it. I got: 'Oh, yes, well — can I tell you how much it is first?' And I was a little bit offended that he might have thought I couldn't afford it. But good on him for making sure he was not wasting his time.

There have been times when we have done an arrangement and people said money was not an issue. Then they got the bill and it was a big issue. So that's why we say it up front. It is more respectful to tell them upfront than make them embarrassed or see them in financial difficulty later.

Times are tough enough as it is, so they need to know if what we do will be outside their budget. It's like anything you buy. If the TV at Harvey Norman is too expensive, go to The

Warehouse. If you have the money for a Honda, you should buy a Honda not a Mercedes. There is nothing wrong with Hondas. They are very reliable.

We don't say no to anyone, but we might suggest a different sort of funeral than what they were thinking of.

Covid has changed this a bit. People got a fright about their finances. Now when I say, 'Can we talk about costs?' people say, 'Yes, please, that is something we really want to know about.'

Pākehā are a bit different. They just want the account at the end, and I love that, too.

Everyone is treated the same. We still require the deposit and will give the invoice on this date. We send it to the lawyer for Pākehā families because it is usually coming out of the estate. But for Māori families we have time payment. At other Māori-run funeral businesses I've been involved in, they were very relaxed and didn't bother with a deposit. But since we have brought this in, all the Māori funeral homes are doing it. It is tough but we need to do it to survive.

* * *

There is a lot of discussion about Pākehā taking over bits of Māori culture. This comes up at work. I have a responsibility to tell people the best way to do things and sometimes what they want might not be appropriate. I will listen to their wishes for their mother's tangi and I might say: 'We can do A and C, but B is a bit distasteful.' It's the same as with a tā moko. Some designs are suitable and some are not. A tā moko artist might say the same thing if you go to him with a design you want. He can do A and

B, but C isn't appropriate. They will make sure everything is done properly.

I think a lot of big companies understand they have to get with the programme. They can't keep ignoring Māori culture. They have to make tikanga part of what they do.

Usually, I love it when I see Pākehā businesses branding themselves with Māori names or motifs. Moko are a big example of that happening, especially when you have music stars like Robbie Williams using our designs. I'd much rather see our culture being used than not.

I don't mind businesses giving themselves Māori names if they do it the right way. They should just get help to make sure they have the words right and don't misuse the patterns. I recommend all non-Māori get advice first. It is very easy to access the right information now, especially with social media.

The danger is that a Pākehā person could get something Māori awfully wrong, then other countries get hold of it, because everything is so accessible, and soon it is all over the place.

I saw Kim Kardashian getting her kids to do a haka. That was amazing. A lot of people put it down, but it is our culture being seen on a global stage. They are not Māori, but they did the best they could. The fact she knows about Aotearoa and haka is amazing.

The haka can survive that sort of treatment. I encourage anyone, especially when they are going to put something on social media, to get it as right as you possibly can. Because it will probably not be just for your family to watch. Someone overseas misinterpreting it would be a pity. I know mistakes will happen but if people ask first, there won't be as many mistakes, and it matters that it comes from a good place in their heart.

I notice in the news when people are criticised for misusing Māori names and designs, they often say, 'We didn't know who to ask.' You can always ring the funeral home and ask us. I don't want to be the Māori who is complaining about what people do, but the one who will be there to help people do the right thing.

THIRTY

RELIGION

You have to understand other religions if you are going to look after people in death. You have to have an open mind to everyone's understandings or beliefs.

FRANCIS

Religion is important in my work and in my life. You have to understand other religions if you are going to look after people in death. You have to have an open mind to everyone's understandings or beliefs. It is not a job in which I can insist people respect my beliefs. I have to set aside my personal preferences. I may be asked to do things that are not in line with how I was brought up. It's not about me. It is about the whānau and about love.

I used to find it challenging when I met people who didn't want anything to do with religion.

When I go to uplift someone from their family home, it feels incomplete if it is not accompanied with a karakia.

'Shall we have a karakia now?'

'No, we're okay, thanks.'

And I used to be a bit shocked, but I would have to go with it.

As a funeral director, I encounter all kinds of beliefs. Some are very strange to me, but who am I to even have an opinion about what anyone else should believe?

Sometimes, I sit at a funeral listening to the rituals that are being performed by all the different religions. It makes me reflect on life after death and, whoever it is, I always find myself thinking: 'They've got some good points.' Perhaps it is just the mood I am in.

Ultimately, the beautiful thing about it is that it all comes to a place of a higher being. If you climb up the ladder far enough, there is that matua nui i te rangi who connects everyone.

I find it really easy to adapt my thinking to the different words and beliefs in the funeral service. If we take the time to understand, it seems to me that all religions make sense. Funerals give you that chance to think about those things, whether you are religious or not.

From what I gather, most people don't experience this. They have their way and their beliefs and they are stuck in them. I think I am lucky that my work allows me to have a more open mind. I see the different beliefs working and doing the same job for everyone.

It's not going to make me change my own religion. It's going to do the opposite. If all religions have value for people, then I can be content with my own faith.

I only struggle when there is no faith. There was a case where a family wanted me to be a celebrant. The person had not been a believer and neither were the family. They didn't want any prayers. That was on the notes they gave me: no prayers, no religion, no mihi — because that means Heaven.

They gave me a wonderful poem to read out called 'The Devil's Train', which had the Devil speaking. That was the most difficult thing I've ever done because it was so hard for me not to bring God into it somewhere. I googled a lot to help me construct a memorial without religion. Now I can add to our Tipene Funerals kaupapa: Atheists Served Here.

When it is an atheist funeral, I know it is their belief and what they want and I respect that, but for my own sanity I say a little prayer to myself. It is for me, not for the mate. When you are working with another's religion, or none at all, it's good to hang on to a little bit of what you believe.

It has probably been more of a shock to me because growing up I wasn't exposed to any other religions. I had no acquaintance with Rātana and Ringatū until I entered the world of funeral directing. I was shocked when I found out Anglican ministers had wives.

At my funeral, I would like to have lots of different faiths participating because there are so many beautiful facets to all of them. I love the band that the Rātana have leading the procession into the cemetery. Everyone knows the drill: the band goes first and the people follow.

In most Māori Catholic funerals, you don't have any accompaniment. So when I went to my first Rātana service and they had that brass band, I got goosebumps.

Ringatū pray and sing in their special way, with lots of te reo Māori and lots of chanting. I feel close to the Anglican faith. The Mormon faith mainly uses the English language but might have a little te reo Māori at the start. Tongan people are often of the Methodist faith and their funerals are next level. If someone in their parish dies, there are so many mats laid out at the cemetery, gazebos and tents. When the hearse arrives at the cemetery gate, a brass band will be there to lead the tūpāpaku all the way to the grave.

Being brought up Catholic means being brought up to think about religion as essential from the start. Catholic and Māori beliefs complement each other.

Te Aho Matua is a belief system that a lot of kura kaupapa run. It includes their founding principles. That is beautiful, too. It is very Māori. I learnt about this and the different gods when I was at training college with Kaiora. It is complicated and includes all the Māori gods — Tangaroa and many others.

After doing some research, it made sense to include all those gods in our prayers because we take from each of them at some point in our life. I believe in God the creator of Heaven and Earth, but these other identities also have meaning for me, even though I might find it hard to explain.

I might look on them as kaitiaki. If I'm out on the water and we catch a lot of fish, I think, 'Tangaroa has looked after us well today.' If we are walking in the bush and there are lots of beautiful birds around, I thank Tāne Mahuta for bringing them to accompany us.

On top of that and dealing with these beliefs, I converted from Catholicism to Mormonism thanks to my wife. I was very attracted by the way Mormonism was about building you up to be a better person or father. It was about keeping your wife happy and preparing you to go to Heaven when the time comes. That really grabbed me.

When I was struggling with my decision, I prayed and asked God for a sign and a beautiful feeling came upon me to say it was right.

I sit at a funeral listening to the rituals that are being performed by all the different religions. It makes me reflect on life after death and, whoever it is, I always find myself thinking: 'They've got some good points.'

Also, although it was very American, it showed a lot of respect for Māoridom. I heard the head of the Mormon church on a broadcast speaking to people in New Zealand. He said when he came here, he heard a hymn that the Māori people sang and it had stayed with him. And I was amazed that he was singing a Māori hymn. I felt like he had connected with us and knew us.

KAIORA

When my dad converted to Mormonism, he went all the way, of course. He drummed into me that I should marry someone who had been on a Mormon mission posting overseas and proved himself.

In Dad's mind, someone who had served their mission would have an understanding of how you treat a woman. He would have good values from understanding the gospel. That is what he wanted for his daughter.

So I didn't do that. None of us married a man who had done a mission. My dad didn't do one either because he was a convert and way too old.

It was very serious for him. When he converted, his family disowned him for some time. The fights over religion continued right up until he was on his deathbed.

Dad loved to read. He was self-taught and a great student. He always read the scriptures. He read the newspaper every day. He read lots of books.

And one day he opened his mind up to the Book of Mormon. He decided to see for himself what all this was about, and he read the whole thing. At the end, he had some sort of revelation telling him to join the church. It was not forced on him.

His mother was so hurt. His siblings ganged up on him: 'How can you do this to our mother?'

My mother was hurt, too. She was the Mormon, so she felt responsible, even though she hadn't done anything to try to convert him.

Eventually, his mother came to understand his decision. He was her son and he could do what he wanted, including having his own little revelation, just for him.

For Francis and me, our Mormon faith has given us values that we have learnt out of the Gospel. If we don't go to church as much as we should or follow some teachings all of the time, the faith is always there.

Even though I'm less active, I still know deep down those Gospel principles that can help me. When someone in our work asks us to have karakia, that is me — I am in there. I am in tune with that. As a child growing up, prayers in the morning and in the evening with our dad were the norm. If we missed karakia in the morning, we felt something was wrong all day. If we were out and it was time for karakia, Dad pulled the van over: 'Who is going to say prayers for us?'

Our big boy is fifteen now and can make his own decisions about these things. I know Francis would not be happy if any of our boys ended up having no faith. He thinks that it is important to have a spiritual aspect in your life. It is important for me, too, but I couldn't force anyone to do it or have it.

He expresses it by saying that through our life, we work, we have a husband or wife, then kids and hopefully some beautiful times. Then we are put in a box and burnt or buried. To Francis, there has to be a reason for doing all this and only the spiritual

Papatūānuku is part of my spiritual life. She is beautiful to me — the epitome of all wāhine atua.

dimension can provide that reason. It is very important to him that all our children understand that there is something more than just what we can see around us.

As a child, I wasn't given the agency to make a decision about going to church or not. It was forced on me. That was how it was, and I didn't mind that. I'd love it if my son served a mission, and he knows that, but I won't force him.

I have some really good friends who served the mission and loved it. I admire how staunch they were to do that. Women can do it too now, and I wish I could have gone when I was young.

My father took missionaries with him to the marae. It wasn't always straightforward. They were not always invited and they were not always welcome. Sometimes they were turned back: 'Hani, don't bring your Mormon tikanga here.'

But it was a bit like a special project for my dad — his own personal mission. He was keen to take them on. He told them what to do, guiding them through the process. Then he would get up and have a mihi, all in te reo Māori. 'Look, you fellas know me. I am of this faith,' and he would preach to them for as long as they would let him, and get the men who had done the mission to talk about their work.

Mormonism and Māori are a good fit because they share a tikanga. The values around family are very similar.

You can't generalise and say Māori are a deeply spiritual people or that we all share a religious outlook. But I think it's fair to say that most do. I have some staunch Māori friends who are not religiously open. I know some who prefer to be tikanga-driven rather than religion-driven. That can be accommodated in our world and in Māoridom.

There is a lot of karakia on a marae and it might not always be to the same god. I think we are praying to the same people, but other people think there is a karakia for Papatūānuku and a karakia for Ranginui and karakia for the Christian God and that they are different karakia. There are so many different karakia that even I struggle to understand a lot of them. There are certain words that are used that I need to learn. Each of those words has a whakapapa and you don't just want to use them loosely. You have to understand each word properly.

Even though I am a Mormon, Papatūānuku is part of my spiritual life. She is beautiful to me — the epitome of all wāhine atua. Some say she is just Mother Earth, but she is more than that and she means a lot to me.

THIRTY-ONE

BUSINESS

The most important thing in life is he tangata, people. It is the most important thing in business, too. It is the relationships you make — the whakapapa there — that are the key to success.

FRANCIS

As the old whakataukī says, the most important thing in life is he tangata, people. It is the most important thing in business, too. It is the relationships you make — the whakapapa there — that are the key to having a successful business yourself and to connecting with other businesses that you will work well with. You can be really flash, or not so flash, with what you provide, but people will come and do business with you if they like you.

At our bank, we get to know the tellers and the manager. They are big corporates but you can still have a personal relationship if you make time for a kōrero and to get to know them.

We have looked after two people from that bank who have died. I was expecting more funerals from the bank but they closed the branch down.

Our funeral home in Onehunga is in an industrial area. Around us there are panelbeaters, a steel engineer, mechanics, bakeries, car yards. Often on a Friday afternoon, the people from the different businesses gather outside for a couple of drinks. It is nice to see them hanging out and chatting about things, whether they drink or not. People benefit from those relationships that form on the street.

I walk past the steel engineer every day and notice how busy they are — and when we needed to have a mortuary bench built in stainless steel, there they were, right next door.

Tikanga comes into play when we choose people to work with. For instance, our lawyer is not Māori, but we clicked with him because he has a small family firm just like ours, so we share a lot of the same values. He was also right next to a casket manufacturer, though that was just a coincidence.

Our accountant has a tikanga in the workplace that is similar to what we have. When she comes in here, the first thing we do is catch up about what has been happening. We hear about her life and children and share our own stories, too. Then I remove myself and leave it to my wife to talk about the money. But first and foremost is the kōrero.

There is no point talking about business if people have underlying problems. If I have a son sick at home and I am rushing to get through things with her so I can get back to him, then it is easy for mistakes to be made. So we talk about those things first, and if we find out there is a problem we can reschedule the meeting.

Survival comes into it too, though, and sometimes we have to put our tikanga on hold to keep the business strong and get to the next level.

I saw women dressed to the nines in their business suits and from a young age that was something I aspired to do. But I didn't think that was possible. I always assumed you needed some great qualification to go into corporate life.

KAIORA

Growing up, I never expected to have a business of my own. In Kaitāia, there is no Glassons or Hallensteins or Seed or Cue. In Kaitāia if you worked at McDonald's, you were the bomb. I always believed a job in fast food or retail clothing was the greatest job you could have.

I saw women dressed to the nines in their business suits and from a young age that was something I aspired to do. But I didn't think that was possible. I always assumed you needed some great qualification to go into corporate life.

I realised you needed experience as well. I could see there were a lot more opportunities in Auckland. For more than a year, nearly two, I applied for jobs at Auckland fashion stores and I was declined many times.

So I went to study a diploma in business at Manukau Institute of Technology and completed that. This was at the time Francis was trying to start his business, and I thought it would be good to acquire some theoretical knowledge to support that. It would be a complement to what he was learning by experience.

At MIT, they taught you fundamentals about how a business operates, about different pricing structures and a lot of money things. But they didn't teach you how to set a business up. They didn't teach you about what to do with tax, paying your staff, how to treat your workers. I had no knowledge at all about how to run a business day to day by the time I came out.

I was the only Māori in our class of about fifteen, which meant that if anything to do with Māoritanga came up, I was the one they looked to for advice. Even the tutor asked me to tell him what he needed to know. There was only a small Māori component in the course, and in the end I felt like I was teaching it. It was like an elective that covered things like pepeha and marae etiquette. The tutor thanked me later for helping him and said he appreciated it because he didn't want to disrespect the culture.

Francis and I pretty much both threw ourselves into the deep end with our own business. For me, that is the best way to learn anything.

We didn't realise how much we didn't know. Then we started to get emails about being behind in payments and we had our accountant telling us there was an IRD payment coming up and asking if we had set aside funds. What? Oh, dear.

Then we had to change a few things and Francis had to learn you can't just buy things all the time. I had to introduce him to the idea of a budget — this is what we have and this is what needs to be paid and this is what we have left over that you can spend and it isn't very much.

We had to change our mindset towards how we got people to pay us, too. First me, then Francis. At the start, we were all about manaaki, and we like to think we still are, but aroha is not going to continue to keep these doors open. If we don't get paid, we can't pay our staff.

I had to push Francis to start asking people for a deposit. He wouldn't do it. If they couldn't pay $800 upfront, which is how much we started asking for, then it would be a struggle to pay more later. We would rather not deal with debt. But now it is the deposits that are keeping us going.

It has been a massive lesson for whānau that engage with us.

'Do we have to pay that?'

'Your mum needs a casket, right?'

At the start, we were all about manaaki, and we like to think we still are, but aroha is not going to continue to keep these doors open.

'Yeah.'

'That needs to be paid for.'

'Really?'

They are in their grief and the last thing they are thinking about is having to pay for things. So we have to prepare them. They have to pay for the marae. Have to pay for kai. For the casket. For the celebrant.

And if we waited for all our payment until the work had been done, we would find that they would rather spend it on something else than use it to pay for Mum's funeral, which they had already had. It has been an interesting journey getting Francis this far. I am grateful for where we are now.

People are changing. A lot more whānau are signing up for prepaid funerals. But that brings up another lesson in a few cases. They believe because they have paid us, they can get it all back. They will start making their payments and be doing really well. Then in eight or nine months: 'Oh, sis, I'm wanting to know if I can get a withdrawal because I have to pay for something else.'

They think we are a bank. We don't hold all their money. We will give them a percentage back, keep a percentage for admin. Not many people have done this. But for those who have, we have told them not to come back.

We don't want to be a bank and we don't want to be a debt-collection agency. We want to be a business that helps people.

As we got bigger, and couldn't be at four funerals in a day, we needed to employ staff. And we have done it according to our tikanga.

I think we've managed well. When we first took people on, the most important thing was whether they could handle the time commitment and sacrifices that come with the role. Funeral directing is not nine to five. People die at all hours. We could work on the other qualities later.

We were never taught how to manage people, so I can only base the way I behave as a boss on how I would like to be treated. We don't have a uniform. We like everyone to dress similarly but with their own style. We have never had to tell anyone what to wear.

If someone came to me and said they had to resign immediately, I would be really upset. What is wrong? Is it work? Is it home? If it's home, how can we help? I take it personally when any staff member is upset. We like to believe we can have a hui or kōrero if there are any issues at all. Often, they are so small and need addressing right away so that they will stay small. If the majority are complaining about something, you have to have a hui. If just one person is complaining, you can kōrero with the one person.

One thing I did learn from business school was very simple: if you want people to be good to you, you have to be good to them. Once I got that, I felt like I had completed the course. And this is what it means if you treat your staff like whānau. After all, they are like whānau. You will spend the majority of your day with them. You have to appreciate and care for one another or it won't work.

THIRTY-TWO

TE TIRITI

It would be good if Pākehā were as aware of the Treaty of Waitangi as Māori are, and able to understand that when Māori protest about the Treaty it is for a really good reason.

KAIORA

Awareness of the Treaty of Waitangi was very much part of my life growing up. We regularly visited the marae at Waimanoni. At these whānau gatherings, we caught up with Uncle Hone, his wife Whaea Hilda and Uncle Mangu. They were all part of the political group Ngā Tamatoa.

They are well known as staunch activists for our people. They have been seen making their points forcefully on TV many times over the years. It wasn't like that when we were with them, but you knew they had strong views about what was right. That was where I learnt a lot of what I needed to know about the Treaty. Away from there, our father taught us his view and we got an understanding of why Hone and Hilda were so strong.

My father had so much respect for them. Hilda is my blood — her mother and my father are first cousins. But we were taught to call Hone Uncle Hone.

Tikanga

At first, all I knew about the Treaty was that there was a partnership and it needed to be enforced.

Dad explained it to us this way: 'It is like me saying I will give you a lolly if you do something for me, and you say okay. Then you do it, but I don't give you the lolly.'

'That's not fair,' we said. 'You can't keep the lolly.'

'Well, that is how it is,' said Dad. 'We signed an agreement and we did what we said we would, but we didn't get the lolly.'

As a child, for me, lollies were gold. Dad didn't buy many things. We couldn't afford them and if we had any at all we had to share them. So there was always a worry in the back of my mind that if someone promised something they might renege. Even now, I am cautious if someone offers me something. I worry about them reneging. I won't take anyone's word for it until it happens. They laugh about it at work because if someone says they are bringing a cake tomorrow, I don't believe them until I see the cake.

What happened with the Treaty was always there as part of Dad's mental background. His mother, Nana Katie, was very staunch. He learnt a lot of tikanga, history and whakapapa from her. But he also loved to read and had all these books by people like Elsdon Best and Māori Marsden. My dad and Māori Marsden's wife were first cousins. He would share views with these people. You could see them on the taumata or go to a whare where they would all sit together. I just wanted to go out and play, and when I got tired and went back inside, they would still be going. They never even seemed to get up to go to the toilet. Now I wish I could have been part of those conversations. I wonder what they had to share.

Dad would do his best to be an activist when he could, and it frustrated him when he got sick and couldn't do as much.

I wasn't taught anything about the Treaty at school or intermediate. It wasn't till I got to Unitec to learn tikanga — it was a compulsory paper — that I really got to study it. When they went into detail about it, we felt hurt for our people from those times.

I didn't really like learning about it because it brought back so much bad feeling. We need to accept it has happened if we are going to fix things. We need to accept the language was different in each version and each party agreed to something different. I believe that is why Uncle and his whānau are so strong about this.

I also learnt more about the Treaty in a law paper I did once. There was maybe one lecture in a whole course. It was a big lecture theatre with a couple of hundred people there.

'Where do you think we went wrong with the Treaty?' the lecturer asked. He was Pākehā and I thought it was interesting he said 'we'. I thought he was referring to him and his people. I was looking around thinking: 'Am I the only Māori in this room?' No one said anything.

'The language,' I yelled out. 'The language is the biggest problem.'

'Points on!' he said. Yay.

He highlighted the differences in the people who signed the Treaty between the number of Māori people who understood te reo Māori and the number who understood English. Then there are parts in the Treaty that weren't correctly translated into te reo Māori. Some of the chiefs may not have understood what they meant.

That is why he asked everyone what they thought the problem was. He had already explained to us that all our tūpuna understood te reo Māori. Maybe a few understood a bit of English — that was just coming in.

The history is that it was a formal legal document at some point, recognising a true partnership. Then a court case came along fighting over whenua and a judge made it a precedent to become a simple nullity.

A lot of people went quiet then. I could feel that from the people in this room there was some respect for what took place.

I didn't want to be in that class anymore. I didn't go to any of the tutorials because I knew if I did it would lead to a heated discussion with a random person I had never met before and I didn't want to use that kind of energy. All that, and we only touched on the Treaty once.

We are seeing the Treaty working in some areas now. When Uncle Hone got into Parliament and was sworn in, he read it all in te reo Māori. (Then he was booted out.) I thought, 'That is you, Uncle. You are so staunch.' I don't think he would get booted out today. But when Rawiri Waititi made his speech in te reo Māori in 2021 there was yet another fuss.

It is funny that we have this Treaty in English and Māori, yet in the 1980s we had to pass a special act to make te reo Māori an official language for this nation.

Our kids will grow up understanding more than we did at their age. When Moronai was eight or nine, he was all about Māori rights. The first year our family went to campaign for Peeni Henare, he was the only one who would not wear a Labour Party T-shirt like all the rest of us. He wore a Mana Party shirt.

'Where did you get that?'

Dad explained it to us this way: 'It is like me saying I will give you a lolly if you do something for me and you say okay. Then you do it, but I don't give you the lolly. Well, that is how it is. We signed an agreement and we did what we said we would, but we didn't get the lolly.'

'Aunty gave it to me. I just don't want to wear what you fellas got.'

'Why not?'

'I just don't think they are for the Treaty.'

My sister. Thanks a lot.

'Look, Mum's not going to tell you to take that off, but if you come with us there may be people who will give you flak for wearing that.'

'Sweet.'

Oh my gosh, my son! I said he was allowed to express what he believed, and he did. I was so proud of him.

Some months after the election, we had a whānau reunion. Francis got up and did a mihi and shared the story of what Moronai had done.

'Where are you, nephew?' called out Uncle Hone. 'I need to give you a big mihi. Come and give your Uncle Hone a big hug.'

Some businesses have official Treaty policies. We don't but as an employer I feel I have a responsibility to staff to educate them if they are not aware of it. We operate on the principles of tiaki, manaaki. I feel that if I'm speaking te reo Māori, I am actually being an activist for the Treaty. If I am speaking it in a room where there are people who may not know any te reo Māori at all, I feel just a little bit that I am exercising something to do with Treaty rights.

FRANCIS

We learnt about the Treaty at school. At primary, we were taught about the two versions of the Treaty and what a partnership is and how we should have equal rights at the table.

The main things for us in the north, when I was at school, were to do with the Department of Conservation. It was important for them to work with iwi. That was a good example of the Treaty working. You had a government department saying: We need to have a worker with the iwi. Is it okay to come on the land, okay to go this way, how we are going to protect the whenua and the trees?

Whaea Pani would bring it up. 'We are going to a hui today about 1080 and because of the Treaty we are working together — a government department and us as a people.' We thought that made sense. The hui were really boring but it was a good example.

Māori probably think about and talk about the Treaty more than a lot of people realise. Even in kapa haka, for instance. We used that a lot to express feelings about what had happened. You will hear it at every kapa haka event. Most groups would sing about things such as patu tikanga, where you disrespect tikanga. They call it tāhae taonga — stealing precious things. My aunty wrote a song about that when I was growing up, and nearly all my cousins know this song.

Now the Treaty is a natural part of our working life. For me, the most important thing is making our tamariki aware of it. We work and want to live in both worlds. As soon as our kids step away from the immediate environment we have created for them and get a real job and do real hours, then they will understand a lot more about the need to make sure the Treaty is upheld. There is a long way to go. When I read about what big corporates are doing now around the Treaty, and how they are trying to bring knowledge of tikanga into their work, making everyone aware, I always think it is beautiful.

Because my wife is a Murray, if there is anything that she thinks is unfair, she pops up straight away. For me, it is more about trying to get through life day by day and focusing on the future for our kids.

Maybe if the Treaty was being observed and working properly, we wouldn't even have to think about it. But for Māori to get a share in decisions, we have had to work really hard and stand up and point to the Treaty.

Also, we want sovereignty, but we have to be able to run our own backyards first. Here's a raruraru. If our people were given a lot of money and the power to run things, it might be different. We wouldn't have issues if there was a real partnership.

There are some iwi who do really well and have good systems in place. You can tell the iwi who are well educated because they are successful. You have to treat your rūnanga and your iwi as a business for them to grow. Once it gets going, you can skim the cream and share it with the people, but we never get to see the cream because it is spent before we see it and we get the milk at the bottom of the barrel.

It would be good if Pākehā were as aware of the Treaty as Māori are. It would be good to have it taught in all schools so kids understand it. When Pākehā see protests at Waitangi, I hope they realise they are for a really good reason.

Waitangi Day is not really a day to celebrate. It is a day when grievances are brought up. As well as a holiday, we have to remember that the injustices since the Treaty have been huge. Whether you are a businessperson, a school teacher, a boss or employer, see what you can do to honour the Treaty.